Lose Your
Mummy
Tummy

Lose Your
Mummy
Tummy

Julie Tupler, RN

with Jodie Gould

Da Capo
∞
LIFE
LONG

**A Member of the
Perseus Books Group**

Many of the designations used by manufacturers and sellers to distinguish their products are claimed as trademarks. Where those designations appear in this book and Da Capo Press was aware of a trademark claim, those designations have been printed with initial capital letters.

Copyright 2005 © by Julie Tupler with Jodie Gould

Printed in the United States of America.

Da Capo Press is a member of the Perseus Books Group

Credits:
Photos: M G Vander Elst
Illustrations: Kevin Pyle

Set in 12-point Bembo

First printing, 2005

A CIP catalog record for this book is available from the Library of Congress.
ISBN 0-7382-0981-3

Visit us on the World Wide Web at http://www.perseusbooks.com

Da Capo Press books are available at special discounts for bulk purchases in the U.S. by corporations, institutions, and other organizations. For more information, please contact the Special Markets Department:

Special Markets Department
Perseus Books Group
11 Cambridge Center
Cambridge, MA 02142
(800)-255-1514
specialmarkets@perseusbooks.com

I did not want to leave this planet without hearing someone calling me "mom." So I dedicate this book to my daughter, Florencia, who gives me strength when I am weak and has taught me what really matters in life. In her eyes I can see a reflection of who I am and who I want to be.

— J.T.

To my beloved daughter Samantha, who has shown me how to see the world as a place of joy and wonder. And to my husband, Robert Katel, who helped bring her into our lives.

— J.G.

Table of Contents

Preface

AS MUCH FUN AS I HAVE HAD being a model and actress, I've always known that being a mother is my true calling. So when I learned that I was pregnant with my first child, I was ecstatic. I was seven months pregnant with Flynn when I started training for my upcoming labor with Julie Tupler. I say "training" because, as a runner, I've always been health- and fitness-conscious, and I knew that I had to prepare both physically and mentally for what Julie calls "the marathon of labor."

I worked with her several times a week during the last six weeks of my pregnancy, in addition to swimming and doing some modified yoga. Although I started late in my first pregnancy, the Tupler Technique abdominal exercises I learned for pushing and preventing back problems really worked! Julie designed a pregnancy-fitness workout that strengthened my back and abdomen for delivery. Understanding how to push with strong transverse muscles while relaxing my pelvic floor muscles gave me that mind-body connection so necessary during labor.

A Lamaze class will teach you how to breathe to get through the pain of labor, but the Tupler Technique teaches you how to push and relax at the same time. I don't think Flynn could have been brought into the world with only twenty minutes of pushing without it. I had equally good results with my second delivery. And I'm pleased to report that I did not have an episiotomy in either of my deliveries!

I also feel that Julie's program helped snap me back into shape after giving birth. I needn't tell you how miraculous yet daunting the changes in your body become. Thankfully, any extra baggage you might get when pregnant is only temporary, and that includes the mummy tummy, which you get rid of by doing the Tupler Technique and breast-feeding. I am not an advocate of quick weight loss after a baby and recommend breast-feeding for at least six months. But these few exercises can strengthen your abdomen and pelvic floor from day one.

Motherhood is exhausting enough; you don't need weakened stomach and back muscles to make the job harder! New moms must learn how to move around safely, especially when doing the day-to-day stuff like getting up, sitting down, picking up a baby, or picking up after him.

As a woman, you don't want to replace your entire wardrobe because you've gone up two sizes. The good news is that your body *will* repair itself, and you can get even stronger by doing the Tupler Technique exercises every day and by eating the proper diet. Not only will your mummy tummy go away, that aching baby back will also disappear. For women who didn't exercise before pregnancy, the Tupler Technique will make you look and feel better than you did before your pregnancy. You may not feel like a supermodel, but you'll sure feel like a super mom!

—Elle Macpherson

Foreword

I HAVE KNOWN AND WORKED with Julie Tupler since the conception of Maternal Fitness (a labor-preparation program that features the Tupler Technique) in 1990. Over the years, I have sent my pregnant patients to her classes and have seen the results. Women who do their exercises regularly and use the Tupler Technique effectively have healthier pregnancies, quicker deliveries, and easier recoveries after childbirth.

Those who continue the program after childbirth continue to improve. Strengthening the abdominal muscles gives support to the back, which helps ease the stresses of motherhood by preventing injury during the lifting, reaching, and carrying that come with the territory. Improved posture helps new mothers look and feel their best while losing the residual pregnancy pounds. Restoring the tone of pelvic floor muscles reduces the risks of incontinence and improves bowel, bladder, and sexual function. The return of a flat tummy and a tight pelvic floor are great tonics to self-esteem. Even those who get a late start—five, ten, or twenty years after their last deliveries—can benefit from the exercises in this book.

Julie's Maternal Fitness program makes my job easier and it can make motherhood easier for you. Practice these exercises daily and follow the safety tips carefully to get the full benefits of this program.

—Gae Rodke, OB-GYN

Introduction

CONGRATULATIONS ON HAVING COMPLETED one of the most thrilling (and challenging) experiences of your life! After nine months of carrying another little being, you finally have your body back to yourself. But somehow you're not the same as you were before you became pregnant. You're exhausted, for one thing—not just tired but mommy-tired. You might have pain in your shoulders and lower back. Your breasts are probably so swollen that they feel like they belong to someone else (which they kind of do, if you're nursing). Your wrists might ache a little and you might feel some numbness in your hands. If you've had an episiotomy, it's difficult to sit comfortably or to go to the bathroom. Perhaps even more horrifying is the discovery that you've gone up several dress sizes!

Don't despair. I'm here to tell you that you that not only will you get your body back to what it once was, it can be even better than it was pre-pregnancy!

I will show you why my Tupler Technique exercises, which engage the transverse abdominal muscle, are now being used by delivery nurses, midwives, childbirth experts, celebrities, and women all over the world.

Those of you who read my first book, *Maternal Fitness*, are already familiar with how the Tupler Technique helps you push out the baby during labor. This book will show you how this technique will help you now that the baby is born. Once you master the simple steps of the Tupler Technique and follow the advice and exercises I've outlined in this book, you will have:

- A tighter, flatter stomach
- A smaller waistline
- A reduction or elimination of back pain
- The ability to safely lift your baby and heavy objects
- More energy
- Better posture
- The perfect preparation for your next pregnancy!

Working with pregnant and postpartum women is so rewarding because I get to see the difference my exercises make during this exciting time of life. After becoming a registered nurse in Illinois, I moved to California, where I started doing vocational rehabilitation for people with back injuries. I later moved to New York, where I began teaching exercise classes at a health club. The owner there said, "You're a nurse. Why don't you teach our prenatal class?" The idea appealed to me because I had always wanted to work with pregnant women.

When the women in my classes learned that I was a nurse, they started to pick my brain. What would labor be like? How long would it last? How much would it hurt? It had been quite a while since I had done labor and delivery, so I decided to go back and do more research. I became certified as a childbirth educator with Childbirth Education Specialists (CES) and I studied with the International Childbirth Education Association (ICEA).

I was surprised to learn that childbirth-education classes are usually taken at the end of pregnancy. They prepare the mind but not the body for childbirth. Think about it. You wouldn't run a marathon without doing the physical training, would you? I decided that pregnant women needed to prepare physically for what I call the "marathon of labor," and Maternal Fitness was born.

When I started doing my Tupler Technique with the general population more than a decade ago, I found that people's back pain would dramatically lessen or disappear entirely within three days of doing the exercises. It occurred to me that the Tupler Technique would also help pregnant women, who frequently experience back pain caused by the separation of their abdominal muscles and the postural changes that come from carrying the weight of the baby. Almost immediately, pregnant students' backs began to feel better. Even more remarkably, women who used the Tupler Technique were able to push more effectively during labor and recovered faster afterwards.

I also studied with Penny Simkin, a childbirth educator who conducts workshops for doula trainers (labor-support people), so I could attend births. I saw a laboring mom

I had worked with push her baby out so effectively that she almost blew the doctor across the room. I thought, "Oh my God, this really works!"

In the past, pregnant women were told to avoid doing abdominal exercises during pregnancy for fear that it would somehow put pressure on the fetus. Hogwash! That's like the old misconception (no pun intended) that having intercourse during pregnancy will poke the baby in the head. First-time moms and veteran moms who do the Tupler Technique all see a marked difference in their deliveries and postpartum recoveries.

And if this weren't enough, I made *another* exciting discovery. In addition to helping with delivery, back pain, and postpartum recovery, the Tupler Technique actually decreased the separation of the abdominal muscles caused by the growing uterus. This separation, called the diastasis, is what creates that bulging mummy tummy. And if you think you don't have one, think again. Ninety-eight percent of all pregnant women get a diastasis, and most don't even know they have it. My co-author, Jodie Gould, was one of those people. Twenty months after delivering her daughter, she swore up and down that her mummy tummy was gone. Even before I saw her, I guaranteed her that she still had one. Guess who won that bet?

But I didn't stop there. I had all this anecdotal evidence that my exercises were helping women and I wanted scientific proof. Research gathered at my Maternal Fitness studio found that 58 percent of the pregnant women tested were able either to control or reduce the size of their diastasis by using the Tupler Technique for six weeks. Of the postpartum women tested, 62 percent were able to shrink the size of their diastasis. I took these results to the Physical Therapy department at Columbia University, which agreed to conduct an academic study. Sure enough, the 2001 Columbia University study found that women who had completed the Maternal Fitness program did, in fact, have a smaller diastasis than the control group of women who did not exercise during their pregnancy.

Diastasis, schmiastasis, you say. As important as it is to protect your stretched-out muscles, you bought this book because you want to lose your flabby tummy and look better. That's fine with me. I tell my students, "If I don't sell you on the fact that you're not going to have back problems, I'll get you on the vanity." Aside from losing your postpartum aches and pains, you will begin to get your body back into shape. Some of you will be able to put away those maternity clothes in just three weeks!

And whether you're a stay-at-home mom or are juggling mothering and other work, you need energy and a strong physical foundation in order to go about your life. Housework and childcare involves bending down and lifting. If you have other children, you are picking them up or picking up after them. All these activities put a strain on your back and body. I will show you how to use a protective splint while exercising and lifting the baby. (A splint is a piece of fabric that keeps the abdominal separation from getting worse.) And I will teach you about the right and wrong ways of getting up from a back-lying position, because one wrong move or twist can undo all of the work that you've done.

This book will show you how you can start doing my exercises while you're feeding the baby or watching TV. I will tell you what to do and what not to do if you've had a C-section or episiotomy. Doing the right exercises is the best way to take care of yourself while you're taking care of your baby. One high-powered client I trained during pregnancy had a great delivery, but she stopped doing the Tupler Technique once the baby was born. She called me seven years later to say she had "blown out" a disk and wanted to see me again. I'm not saying that you will have a disk problem like she did, but you are certainly putting yourself and your back at risk if you don't keep doing the Tupler Technique after delivery. I have also included a chapter on how to modify your favorite workouts and which activities you should avoid. I will give you the dish on tummy tucks and operations for closing the diastasis, as well as diet and other tips for nursing moms.

Here in New York I frequently run into former clients pushing strollers on the street. When they notice me in my standard uniform of white leotard and leggings, they often flash their pancake-flat tummies. Onlookers must wonder: "Who is that woman in white?"

Your life may have changed irrevocably since having a baby, but your body doesn't have to. By doing the Tupler Technique on a regular basis, you will get rid of that abdominal separation and unsightly mummy tummy. All it takes is a little determination, but what's better motivation than wanting to fit into those jeans again? My former client Elle Macpherson, who wrote the preface to this book, has a stomach so flat you can bounce a quarter off it—two children later. These exercises really work. If you want to see the exercises in action, get the companion video or DVD. Afterwards, if you ever spot me walking down the street in my all-white exercise outfit, make sure to show me your tummy!

—Julie Tupler, RN

Lose Your
Mummy
Tummy

What *Is* a Mummy Tummy?

AFTER THE JOY AND EXCITEMENT of bringing home your brand-new baby begins to subside, you might notice an unsightly bulge in your belly that won't go away no matter how much you diet or exercise. That pooching belly is what I call the mummy tummy (the technical term is *diastasis,* which I know sounds scary, but trust me, it's not fatal). The mummy tummy is caused by the separation of the outermost abdominal muscles during pregnancy. As your uterus expands over the months of pregnancy, your abdominal muscles stretch and spread to make room for it. Unfortunately, the muscle separation that often occurs as the uterus is expanding with the baby doesn't always disappear after you've given birth.

After the birth, your uterus begins to return to its original size, but the surrounding abdominal muscles are still stretched and slack. Plus, the more babies you have, the bigger the separation gets, and the larger the bulge in your belly, the harder it is to get it all back together. This separation is why some pregnant women show earlier with their second child. The widening of these outer muscles leaves an open door for your internal organs to pop out.

Aside from the perpetual pooch, which is bad enough, the diastasis is the major cause of that aching back you might feel during and after your pregnancy. By ignoring an abdominal separation after pregnancy, you are putting yourself at risk for back problems that will only be exacerbated by age. Women with an extreme diastasis are advised to wear a supportive splint after delivery, but wearing a splint will help *all* women who have an abdominal separation, especially when they are exercising, lifting, bending, or wearing a front-loading baby carrier. I will explain what a splint is and how to wear one later on in the book.

Anatomy Is Destiny

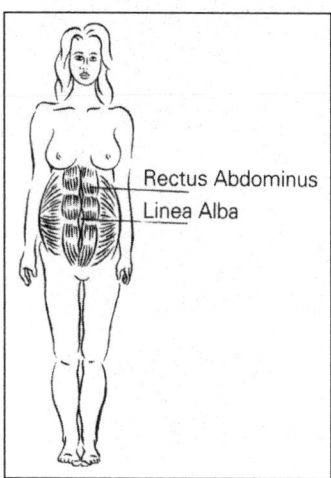

Rectus abdominis: outermost abdominal muscles.

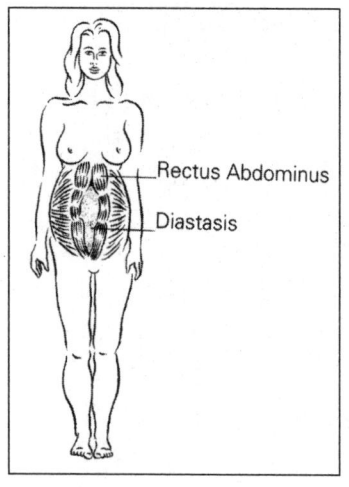

The diastasis. The separation of the rectus abdominis creates a mummy tummy.

As a nurse, it's my duty to give you an anatomical explanation involving some more Latin words, so bear with me. It will help you visualize what's going on inside you.

Many people don't realize that we have three sets of abdominals—the rectus abdominis, the obliques, and the transverse. The rectus abdominis is the outermost muscle that I was talking about earlier. It runs up and down from the sternum (or breastbone) to the pubic bone. It has two halves, called the recti, that are normally about a quarter of an inch apart and are joined together by a fibrous piece of tissue called the linea alba (white line). The linea alba is long and stretchy, like a rubber band. The relaxin hormone that prepares pregnant women for labor by relaxing their joints and muscles also affects the linea alba by making it stretch more easily. As the muscles separate and the linea alba stretches sideways, it becomes thinner, like a piece of plastic wrap covering your organs. This separation is called a diastasis.

The external obliques and internal obliques are the middle layer of the abdominals. The external obliques run diagonally downward from the rib cage to the pelvis; the internal obliques run diagonally upward from the pelvis to the rib cage. The obliques are the muscles that enable you to flex your trunk and turn from side to side. Gym rats who do side-to-side crunches know all about the obliques. Since the obliques are attached to the recti, doing forward-crossover oblique exercises will make the diastasis bigger.

Finally, the transverse muscle (the innermost abdominal muscle) goes straight around the abdomen and back like a corset. It is attached to your bottom six ribs, to the top of your pelvis in back, and to the linea alba of the recti in front. The top of the muscle goes behind the recti and the bottom of the muscle goes in front of the recti. To find this muscle, place your hands on your belly above and below your navel. Take a big breath so that your belly expands. The muscle you feel going out and then in, forward and then backward, is your transverse. Because the transverse is connected to the recti, whenever it goes backwards, the diastasis gets smaller.

The transverse is my favorite muscle. Why do I love it so much? Because doing transverse exercises helps give you that flat stomach we all dream about. It is also the muscle I teach my pregnant students to use while pushing the baby out. Here's the part you new moms will love: The more you work your transverse muscles by doing the Tupler Technique, the faster you'll fit back into your pre-pregnancy clothes. It won't make your skin taut again (how your skin repairs itself depends on age and genetics), but it *will* get rid of your mummy tummy.

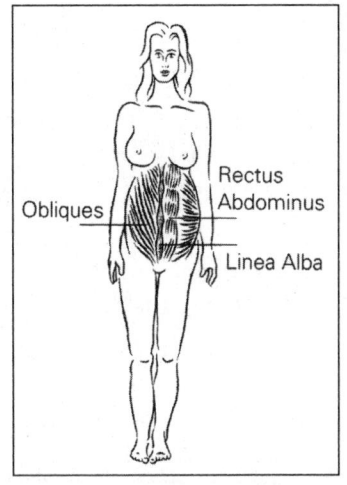

Internal and external obliques are the middle layers of abdominal muscles.

Here's another bonus: When you work the transverse muscle you work four muscles by doing just one exercise! Besides working the transverse, you also work the recti in the front, the lumbar multifidus in the back (the deepest back muscles, which cover the spinal column in your lower back), and the pelvic-floor muscles described below. In other words, when you contract the transverse muscle in the front, you are contracting the back and bottom muscles at the same time. This is called a co-contraction, which has nothing to do with the ones you had during labor!

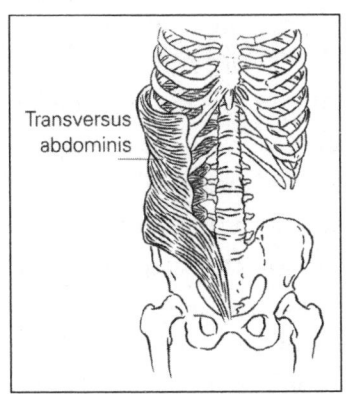

Transverse abdominis (innermost abdominal muscle) attaches in the back to the bottom six ribs and the top of the pelvis.

When I give lectures to women across the country, I make them raise their right hands and swear that their transverse will become their best friend, that they will use this muscle when they get up, lie down, exercise, pick up the baby, and even when they're on the toilet! I firmly believe that the transverse is the missing link in abdominal exercises.

Why should we care about our abdominals? Because the abdominal muscles all help support our backs. We all have a weakness around our bellybuttons, so when you're pregnant the growing uterus presses on this weak area that is now full of relaxin, these muscles

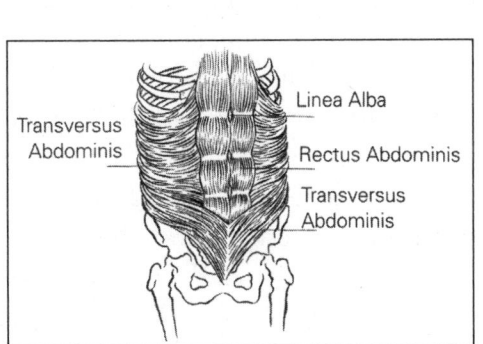

The transversus abdominis comes around from the back and is inserted into the linea alba of the rectus abdominis.

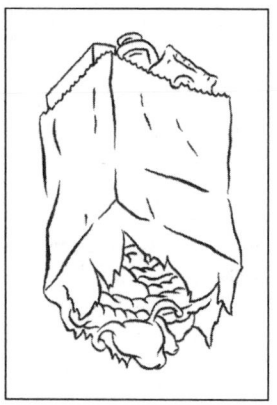

Your pelvis is like a bag of groceries and the pelvic floor is the bottom of the bag.

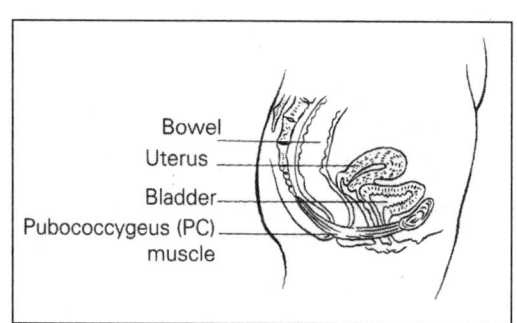

Bowel
Uterus
Bladder
Pubococcygeus (PC) muscle

Side view of the pubococcygeus (PC) pelvic floor muscle.

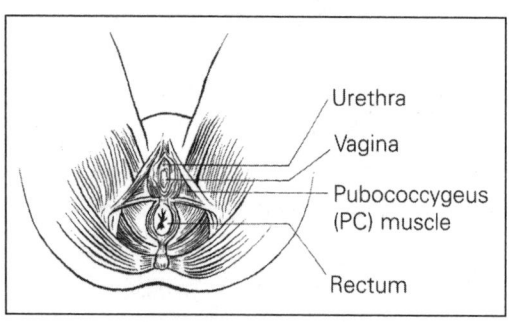

Urethra

Vagina

Pubococcygeus (PC) muscle

Rectum

Back-lying view of the PC pelvic floor muscle.

may separate. Since there are no bones around your belly (such as a rib cage or pelvis, for example), your organs are left unprotected by the separating muscles.

Doing things like getting up from a back-lying position incorrectly or wearing a front-loading baby carrier will make the muscles and tissue spread out even wider (I'll talk about how to avoid this later). The farther apart these abdominal muscles are, the harder it is to get them back together. As a result, your whole internal support system becomes compromised.

Now, while we all want that flat, six-pack stomach, we can't ignore the muscles below the abs, called the pelvic floor. If you think of your pelvis as a bag of groceries, the pelvic floor is the bottom of the bag. For postpartum women, strengthening these muscles means better sex; less or no urine leakage when laughing, sneezing, or coughing; and prevention of what's called a prolapse, where the muscles can no longer support the internal organs. When this happens, the uterus, bowel, and/or bladder may protrude out of the weakened bottom of the grocery bag. As I tell my students, if you don't exercise your pelvic floor, you're going to have a pelvic basement instead.

The main muscle of the pelvic floor, the PC—short for pubococcygeus—lies in a figure eight around the openings to the urethra, vagina, and rectum. The PC is the muscle I tell my students to relax when pushing the baby out. I will show you how to strengthen this muscle later on in the book.

But first, here are some of the most frequently asked questions from new moms about the mummy tummy:

Frequently Asked Questions

How do I know if I have a mummy tummy?

Aside from the bulging belly, you might feel some tenderness around your navel, especially when lifting your baby or transporting her in a front-loading carrier. Your posture may have changed—your belly probably pops out and you might slouch forward to compensate for the lack of strength in your upper back.

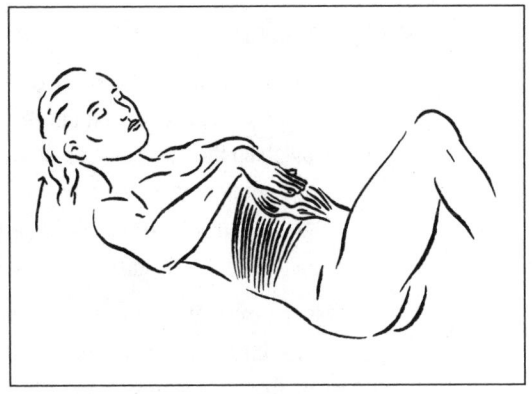

Checking for a diastasis.

Here's how to find out if you have a mummy tummy rather than a plain old flabby belly. Lie down on your back with your knees bent. With your fingers pointing down toward your feet, hold your fingers flat on your belly.

Should I have surgery for my mummy tummy?

From an interview with Dr. Edmund Kwan, MD, Board-Certified Plastic Surgeon with New York Hospital:

- I frequently see patients with mild to severe diastasis. In severe cases the muscles are so weak that the intestines are bulging through the belly like a hernia. When I examine these patients I can put my hand right through to their intestines because they have no muscle. And when I go in during surgery I see a huge weak area.

- You know how when you relax your stomach muscle your tummy sticks out a bit? If you have better tone, your muscles will keep everything from bulging out. Even women who have good muscle tone can get a diastasis when pregnant because the muscles get pushed aside and all you have is the fascia [a cellophane-like covering] holding in the intestines.

- One woman I saw recently [had] had her last child five months before, but still looked like she was pregnant. She was wearing a girdle to keep the bulge in. Many women tell me they are getting back to their pre-pregnancy weight, but they still look like they are pregnant because of this bulge above or around the bellybutton.

- Surgery for the diastasis is different [from] a tummy tuck, which is really three operations at once. In a tummy tuck, we do some liposuction, then raise the skin up to the

(continues)

What Is a Mummy Tummy?

(continued)

ribs just below the breast before tightening the muscle. This is usually with patients without a diastasis. In a diastasis operation, I bring the two muscles together without stitching the muscles themselves. I stitch the fascia that houses the muscles instead. I'm not tightening the muscles, I'm tightening the diastasis. Many insurance companies will pay for diastasis surgery because it's not cosmetic like a tummy tuck. I take photos of the diastasis and send it right to the insurance company.

- I can close the abdominal gap, but if patients strengthen those muscles through exercise their tummies will be even smaller. For a mild to moderate diastasis, patients can do exercises so they won't need surgery. For severe cases, no matter how much exercise you do, you won't be able to close the gap. But for most women, exercise alone will work. I urge my patients to exercise first to see if they can close their diastasis before seeking out surgery.

You need to check in three places: at your bellybutton, three inches above your bellybutton, and three inches below. Press your fingers down as you lift your head (not shoulders) off the ground very slowly. After childbirth, you will feel a gully between the midline of your body. That's the diastasis. The more fingers you can fit in that gully, the worse it is. I've seen women with everything from a two- to a ten-finger separation! If you're having trouble finding your abdominal separation, ask your doctor to check it for you or come to one of my "Lose Your Mummy Tummy" seminars and I will check it for you!

Should I have a doctor check for a diastasis?

While your OB/GYN can check your mummy tummy after childbirth, most doctors will not give you advice on how to repair the separation. By doing a self-exam, like the one I showed you above, you can keep track of your progress as you do my exercises by recording the number of fingers you can fit in the gully.

Won't my mummy tummy go away if I breast-feed?

Breast-feeding does help to shrink the uterus, which will keep it from pressing on that recti muscle and help alleviate some of the pain. But nursing will not help to close the abdominal separation. You must physically exercise the transverse muscles in order to close the diastasis.

Will crunches and crossover sit-ups help close the transverse muscles?

Actually, doing crunches and forward crossovers (where the elbow goes to the opposite knee) for the obliques can make the abdominal separation larger. The fact is, most people do sit-ups and crunches incorrectly. Many people only work the top and bottom of their recti (outermost muscle), letting the middle of the muscle get longer. The most important part of a sit-up is what happens in the middle. If you're not working from the middle, you might as well not crunch at all. I will show you exercises that work your abdominal muscles from the middle, but there are a few things you need to know first:

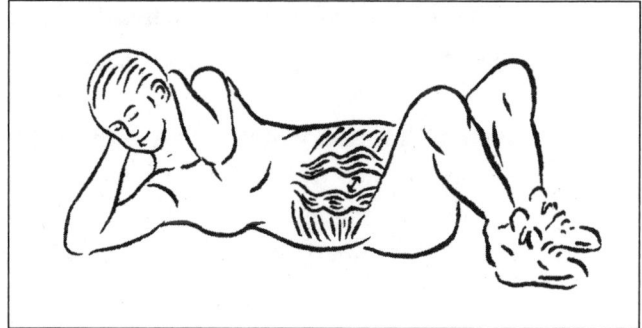

Doing forward crossover oblique exercises will make a diastasis larger.

- **Gravity affects the muscle.** When you do a crunch in a back-lying position, it's very hard to hold the transverse muscle in. This is why I tell my students to start from a seated position. Not only will you get an awareness of this muscle that you have probably never used before, you will have the strength to use it in a back-lying position when gravity makes it harder. This is why you can do the Tupler Technique anywhere, such as on the bus or behind your desk at the office!

- **You must breathe correctly.** When most people do crunches, they breathe and use their abdominal muscles incorrectly. When doing a sit-up, people tend to inhale and suck their muscles in. And when they lift their heads to do a sit-up, they exhale and the abdominal muscles come forward forcefully, making the recti longer in the middle of the muscle and increasing the separation. In learning the exercise that I will show you later, you will see why it is crucial to start with what I call a belly breath, so that the belly is *out* before you start the work and *in* on the work of lifting your head.

- **The higher you lift your head above your hips, the harder it is to engage your transverse**. In fact, it's impossible! That's why doing certain exercises such as the Pilates 100 (where you jackknife your body while pumping your arms one hundred times) will make an existing diastasis bigger or create an abdominal separation if you don't already have one. When postpartum women do crunches, which usually involve lifting the head with hands either on the temples or behind the head, they bring their shoulders and trunks off the floor. This is the worst possible thing for abdominal separation. Using floor abdominizers that automatically lift your head and shoulders when you push down with your arms is just as harmful. If you're going to do a sit-up, only lift your head slightly. If you want to make the exercise harder, instead of lifting your head higher, just move your heels away from your buttocks.

- **The *way* you lift your head is also important**. Never jut your chin out like a turkey while you are doing crunches. Aside from being unattractive, it is impossible to hold your transverse muscle in while your chin is pulled forward. The proper way to lift your head while doing crunches is to nod like you're saying "yes."

- **Pay attention to the direction in which you move your body.** Because the obliques (middle layers of the abdominals) are attached to the recti (outermost muscle), forward–crossover movements make the diastasis larger.

Can people who aren't pregnant have a mummy tummy?

Yes, incorrectly performed exercises, as I explained above, can create an abdominal separation. I'm now training a Pilates instructor who is trying to become pregnant and who has a diastasis from doing the 100s that I talked about earlier. Men and women can get mummy tummies from exercising incorrectly and/or from the constant pressure that is put on these muscles from constipation.

> A good rule of tum: If you can't engage the transverse muscle, you probably shouldn't do it.

Put your hands on your belly again. Take a breath. Now, hold your breath and bear down. Your tummy comes forward, right? Now do it again, only this time take a deep breath and bring your bellybutton to your spine. Hold it there and bear down once again. You see how your tummy stays in? This is the protected position. It's not always pleasant to think about, but it's important to engage your transverse muscle in this way during a bowel movement to prevent hemorrhoids.

In addition, women who had their babies fifteen, twenty, or thirty years ago may still have mummy tummies if they haven't done anything to close them. One of my students brought her mother to my classes so she could learn how to use the Tupler Technique. Her mom was an active grandmother, so she was thrilled to build up the energy and stamina to baby-sit and play with her grandkids.

How long will it take to get rid of my mummy tummy?

It depends on a lot of things, such as whether or not you were exercising before your pregnancy and how often you use the Tupler Technique. It will take longer to bounce back if you didn't do any exercise during your pregnancy. I'm working with a woman who has a huge diastasis and couldn't exercise because she was on bed rest during her pregnancy. She's trying desperately to get rid of her mummy tummy, but it's difficult because her muscles are weak from inactivity. The good news is that she will see a dramatic difference in six weeks—or less, if she is truly committed to my program.

2

Using the Tupler Technique in the First Two Postpartum Weeks

DOCTORS ONCE BELIEVED THAT new mothers should avoid climbing stairs, carrying anything heavier than a baby, and even driving a car for the first two weeks after giving birth. This was the prevailing wisdom until as recently as the '90s. At the same time, we've all heard those mythic tales about women squatting out a baby in a rice paddy and then getting right back to tilling the fields. The truth about when a postpartum woman can begin physical activity depends on each mom's situation, but most healthy women who have had uneventful births can begin doing certain postpartum exercises within twenty-four hours.

This doesn't mean that you should bound out of bed for a five-mile run. I needn't tell you that it takes a lot of energy for the body to recover from the stress of pregnancy, labor, and delivery. As I said, you will probably feel exhausted during the initial postpartum period, which includes a demanding schedule of feeding and caring for that needy little being you created.

It's important, therefore, that you get sufficient rest, hydration, and exercise, which will help your body recover faster and feel more energized. Fortunately, during the first few days after delivery a mom is usually on a hormonal high that helps carry her through this initial stage of motherhood. At the same time, her body immediately begins to repair itself: The uterus and birth canal start shrinking, and the belly begins to flatten out. This gradual recovery process usually takes around six weeks.

But rather than putting yourself on bed rest (which is impossible, anyway), exercising during this time will prevent your muscles and bones from weakening. First, let me be clear about what I mean by "exercising." Exercise can involve stretching your neck, strengthening your abdominal and pelvic floor muscles, and walking. Remember how walking helped when you were pregnant? Well, walking still helps circulate your blood, tone your uterus, and stimulate your bowels and bladder, lowering the risk of postpartum constipation and bladder infection.

As I tell my pregnant students, the Tupler Technique will prepare your body for the marathon of labor. For you new moms, it will also help during the biathlon of motherhood!

Getting Started

As I've mentioned, anyone who has a mummy tummy—which is 98 percent of postpartum women—will need to wear a splint during daily activities, especially when carrying a baby in a front-loading carrier or sling. The purpose of the splint is to bring together the two halves of the recti, those abdominal muscles I talked about before, which separated during your pregnancy. Wearing a splint will also help remind you to use your transverse muscle.

You can use a scarf or sheet that is approximately five feet long and six inches wide, but I highly recommend using one that is made of a combination of terry cloth and cotton because those materials stretch, making them more comfortable. You can get ready-made cotton and terry cloth splints by going to www.maternalfitness.com, or by calling Maternal Fitness at 212–353–1947. If you are using my terry cloth splint, make sure the terry cloth side is worn next to the skin.

How to wear a splint

I suggest you wear a splint underneath your clothes when you are using a front-loading carrier like the Baby Bjorn and while doing the activities of daily living such as lifting your baby. Put the splint (terry cloth side to your skin) on your back at waist level. Take the right side of it and pull it tightly towards your navel with your left hand. Now take the left side and pull it tightly towards your navel with your right hand. This pulls the two halves of your separated abdominal muscles together. Secure the ends with safety pins to the underlying fabric. Later on, I will explain how to use the splint while doing my exercises.

Resistance Bands

The other thing you will need to get is a resistance band, those wide, stretchy, latex bands that come in different colors depending on the resistance level. You might have used one if you exercised during your pregnancy, or if you've had physical-rehabilitation therapy.

I recommend you start with a medium-resistance band and move on to a heavier-resistance band as you get stronger. You can buy resistance bands at most sporting-goods stores, or you can order them by calling Maternal Fitness or going to www.maternalfitness.com.

A few tips before you start exercising with a resistance band: Examine the band for nicks, small tears, or punctures that may cause it to break. If you find a flaw, discard the flawed band and get a replacement from wherever you purchased it. Store your bands at room temperature in a box, or hang them away from direct sunlight. Long exposure to sunlight may cause damage.

Remove your rings before using the bands and beware of sharp fingernails that might puncture the product. If the band has been tied, untie it before storing. To clean, place the band in a

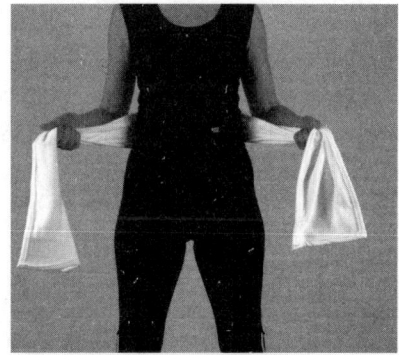

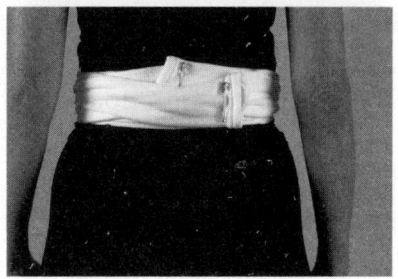

Photo #4: Pin the ends of the splint to the underlying fabric.

container or bag and sprinkle it with baby powder. Stir the baby powder ⸱_
with your hand.

When exercising, remove the slack by grasping with your fingernails.
maintain the natural width of the band. This will prevent it from sliding up ⸱
digging into your hands.

The BAKS Basics:
Easy Moves You Can Do Every Day, Even When
You're Short on Time or Low on Energy

The BAKS Basics are the foundation exercises of my Maternal Fitness progra₁
clude the Tupler Technique abdominal exercises. These exercises can be inc₀
into your daily activities and should be learned before you start your fifteen- and thirty-
minute routines. Most of the BAKS Basics can be done within twenty-four hours of
giving birth. They include the following moves:

Breathing, **B**elly Dancing
Abdominal Work
Kegels
Squatting, **S**tretching, **S**trengthening

If you didn't do these exercises while you were pregnant, I want you practice them
first before you take your exercise routine to the next level. Even if you never take your
exercise regimen to a higher level than BAKS, you'll still be doing your body a great
favor. So let's get started!

Breathing

I know it sounds ridiculous to call breathing an exercise because it's something we do
all the time. Yet we don't always breathe correctly, so we need to practice doing it right.
If you took Lamaze training you know how important certain breathing techniques
were during labor. Well, it's equally important to breathe correctly when you exercise.
Correct breathing is *diaphragmatic*, which means taking air in and out from the diaphragm (not the contraception device, but the part of the belly right below the ribs).
As anyone who has taken yoga will tell you, controlled breathing can be an exercise in
relaxation.

I dislike the word "inhale" because it promotes a tendency to suck in the gut. You should do that when you exhale. Instead, I will instruct you to take "belly breaths," which I will explain below.

Belly Breaths

The belly breath improves circulation, promotes relaxation, prevents breathlessness, and gets the maximum amount of oxygen into your body. Above all, it helps you to work your abdominal muscles correctly.

Sit in a chair or cross-legged on the floor with your back against the wall, and put your hands on your belly. Pretend your lungs are in your belly. Expand your belly as you take air in through your nose and fill your lungs. Watch your belly get bigger. From here on in, this is what I mean when I tell you to "take a belly breath." Exhale through your mouth and empty your lungs as you bring your belly back toward your spine.

Starter's tip: Practice relaxed belly breathing right before you go to bed. When you begin practicing belly breathing you may feel light-headed because you're not used to getting so much oxygen. If this happens to you, breathe in a more shallow way until the feeling passes, or cut down on the amount of time you spend doing belly breaths.

Starting position for hands above knees pelvic tilt.

Belly Dancing

Belly Dancing Exercise #1. Stand with your knees bent, legs apart at hip distance, and your hands, arms, and upper body resting on your thighs above your knees, with no pressure on your kneecaps. Think of sticking out your buttocks to flatten your back.

Think of your recti as a string attached to your pubic bone. Now pull that pubic bone towards your bellybutton to stretch your lower back. Hold for a count of five, and return to center, or to a flat back. Do 10 tilts at a time, at least once a day.

Lengthen or stretch just your lower back.

Starting position for belly dancing on all fours.

Lengthen or stretch only your lower back.

If you have wrist problems, put your fists on the floor instead of your hands.

Starter's tip: Your knees should stay still! Don't move them as you tilt the bottom of your pelvis forward and back to center. Only the pelvis moves. Keep your arms steady and don't use your upper back. Only the lower back is stretching.

This exercise relieves stress on the lower back and prevents backaches.

Belly Dancing Exercise #2: Belly Dancing on All-Fours. Get down on all-fours with your palms flat on the floor, knees hip-distance apart, and toes touching the floor. Keeping your entire back flat and your upper back still, pull your public bone toward your bellybutton to stretch your lower back. Imagine that there is a string attached from your abdominal muscles to your pubic bone. Now pull your pubic bone toward your bellybutton to stretch your lower back. Do 10 tilts at least once a day. If you have wrist problems, you can put your fists, rather than your palms, on the floor. Remember, you are only stretching your lower back, so be careful not to round your upper back.

Abdominal Work

Now we can get to my favorite muscle, the transverse. Locate it by standing up straight and spreading your fingers above and below your bellybutton. Take a belly breath. The muscle you feel moving out and then in as you exhale is your transverse. As I said earlier, the Tupler Technique is based on the connection between the innermost abdominal muscle (transverse) and the outermost muscle (rectus).

The first thing you must do, even while you are still in the hospital, is to strengthen the transverse by doing the two exercises below. Later on, you can incorporate transverse exercises into the fifteen- and then thirty-minute total-body workout. Think of the transverse muscle as a sideways elevator with six floors filling the space between your bellybutton and a parallel point on your back, and your bellybutton as the engine that moves the transverse muscle back toward the spine. On the first floor, your bellybutton is in a relaxed position. If you moved your bellybutton to your spine, you would be at the fifth floor. At the sixth floor, it would feel as if your bellybutton were pushing out of the back of your spine.

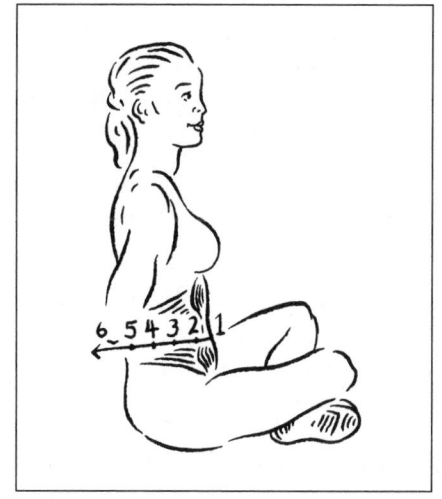

Imagine this muscle is like a sideways elevator with six floors.

Think of going from the fifth to the sixth floor. It's not difficult, but, like any exercise, it takes some practice.

Here are two different ways to do the Tupler Technique:

Seated Tupler Technique. One of the best times to start doing the Tupler Technique is when you're nursing or bottle-feeding; this way, in the beginning, you'll have an automatic reminder to do them every two hours. Some women might prefer scheduling their exercise periods when they are not with the baby so they can give themselves a break and some mommy time. Doing the Tupler Technique during this time allows you to concentrate on yourself, and, above all, to relax. Giving yourself some time away from the baby, and making sure that you take good care of your own needs, will keep you from feeling overwhelmed and exhausted.

Sit in a chair with a seat that is the length of your thighs and buttocks. The seat cushion should be firm, but comfortable. If there are armrests, they should be slightly higher than the bottoms of your bent elbows, so your shoulders don't droop. For all of the seated exercises described below, sit with your butt touching the back of the chair. Ideally, the back of the chair should support your spine; if your chair doesn't fit just right, you might want to place a pillow at your lower back. A low footstool can also be used to maintain that comfortable L-position. Place enough cushions on your lap that your baby is high enough that you don't have to bend forward to feed her.

Babies enjoy the motion created by the transverse exercises because it is the same side-to-side movement they experienced in utero while you were walking. If you're breast-feeding for fifteen minutes on each side, you can do a few sets of transverse exercises while feeding on one side, and some Kegels on the other (see the section on Kegels later in this chapter). If you're using a bottle, switch exercises when the baby is halfway through the feeding.

The more you exercise, the faster your recovery. Remember to drink lots of fluids and to eat at regular intervals, especially if you're nursing.

Elevators.   Sit in a chair or in a cross-legged position on the floor, with your back against the wall and your shoulders lined up with your hips. The purpose of having your back supported by a wall or chair is to keep it steady during the exercise. Once you strengthen your transverse muscle you can do this exercise without the support of a chair or wall.

Put both hands flat on your stomach. Take a belly breath by taking air in through the nose and expanding your belly to the first floor; then bring your bellybutton back toward the spine (fifth-floor position). As your belly moves back toward your spine, imagine your ribs coming together. Hold there for 30 counts. Count out loud so you don't stop breathing. Now, bring your bellybutton even further back: Imagine you are bringing it out the back of your spine (sixth floor). Think of it as just a little squeeze or tightening. Count as you do 5 of these squeezes. End with a deep, full belly breath. Do ten sets every day.

Contractions (drawing in the transverse muscle).   No, these are not those painful things that made you scream while having the baby! Sit against a wall or in a chair in the same position as above. Put one hand above your bellybutton under your ribs (think of your ribs coming together) and one hand below your bellybutton. This is to make sure that both the upper and lower abdominals are moving backwards. Expand your belly and then bring your bellybutton to the third floor (halfway between the first and fifth floors). This is your starting position.

Now, count out loud as you bring your bellybutton to the fifth floor. As it goes back toward your spine, imagine your ribs coming together. This is one repetition. Bring your bellybutton to the starting position at the third floor for the next repetition. Remember to squeeze and hold at the fifth floor. Do not use your shoulders or legs while doing this exercise. You should feel this in your back. The hand on the top should feel the ribs coming together and then going back. It is a common mistake to move the top muscles forcefully forward as the bottom muscles move back; this will increase the diastasis on the top. Thinking about the ribs going back will help prevent a forward movement. Work up to 100 repetitions five times per day. Do two sets of 100 in the morning, two sets before lunch, and one set before going to bed.

After two weeks of doing contractions from the third to the fifth floor, you can then do them from the fourth to the fifth floor. Stay at this level for one week and then progress to working from the fifth to the sixth floor, as in the elevator exercise. Now that your transverse muscle is strengthened, you can start using the splint. When wearing the splint, your abdominal muscles will be closer together at the starting position.

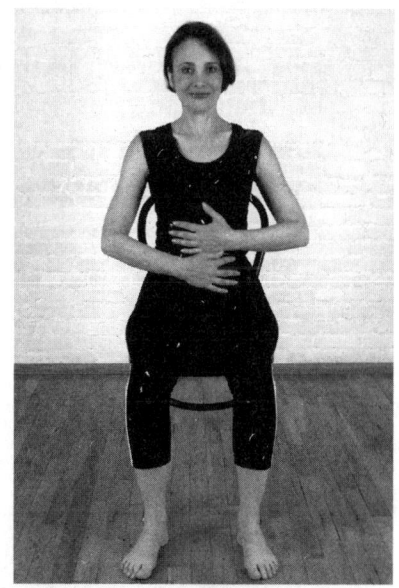

Starting position for the seated Tupler Technique.

Once you master the Seated Tupler Technique, you can continue to do the fifth- and sixth-floor contractions until your child is eighteen years old! You can also increase the number of exercises to ten sets of 100 per day. I know it sounds like a lot, but if you do three sets of 100 in the morning (this should take ten minutes), four sets of 100 before lunch (thirteen minutes), and three sets of 100 in the evening (another ten minutes), it makes it easier to do ten sets per day. That's not a lot of time when you realize that you are not only repairing your body but flattening that mummy tummy!

Back-Lying Exercises

Note: If you have a diastasis, you should always use a splint when doing back-lying exercises.

Pelvic tilt. The pelvic tilt is the foundation for the headlift, and it has three steps. Get in a back-lying position with your legs bent and heels close to your buttocks. One

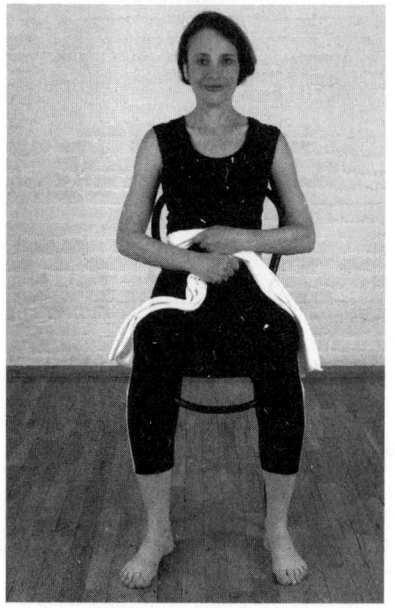

Seated Tupler Technique with splint.

hand should rest on the belly (to make sure you're holding in your transverse) and the other hand should be at your side, by the small of your back, palm facing up (to make sure your lower back is on the floor).

Take a belly breath so that you are at the first-floor starting position. Bring *only* your bellybutton toward your spine. As it moves back toward the fifth floor, imagine your ribs coming together. Be careful not to use your legs when bringing the transverse to the spine. Hold your bellybutton at the fifth-floor position; imagine that you are zipping your bellybutton up to your sternum as you count out loud. This puts the small of your back on the floor. Do not use your legs. Do three sets of ten.

Starting position for back-lying pelvic tilt.

Headlifts. Do not do the headlift exercise until your transverse muscle has been strengthened by doing the seated elevators and contractions, and you can do the back-lying pelvic tilt correctly. Initially, you can do Step 5 without lifting your head. You just bring the transverse from the fifth to the sixth floor. You should use a splint when doing these exercises. Start in the same position as with the back-lying pelvic tilt, only this time holding a splint. Place the splint wherever you have the diastasis, which is different for each individual.

Take a belly breath so that you are at the first-floor starting position. Bring *only* your bellybutton toward your spine. As it moves back toward your spine, imagine your ribs coming together. Do not use your legs to bring your transverse to your spine. Hold your bellybutton at the fifth floor as you imagine that you are zipping your bellybutton up to your sternum. Do not use your legs. Pull the two halves of your rectus abdominis together with the splint. (Each hand pulls toward your bellybutton.) Make sure your hands are on top of your bellybutton so you know that the transverse muscle is not coming out or moving forward. Pressing the back of your neck to the floor, move your bellybutton from the fifth to the sixth floor as you lift only your head as if you were saying "yes" (do not lift your shoulders). Count out loud as you lift your head. Stay at the fifth floor as you put your head down. Start with three sets of 10 and work up to three sets of 30 every day.

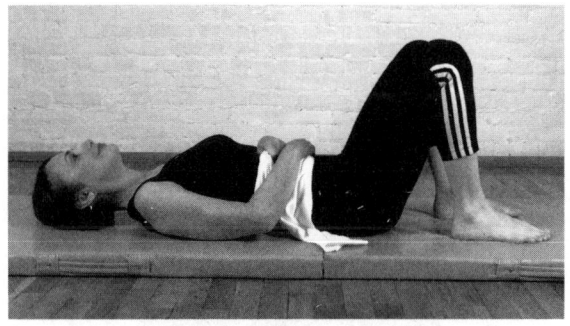

Starting position for head lift.

Lift only your head as if saying "yes."

As you get more advanced, you can make this exercise harder by bringing your feet farther away from your buttocks. The farther away they are, the higher the small of your back comes off the floor. The higher the small of your back is off the floor, the harder it is to use your abdominals to keep it on the floor.

Easiest leg position for headlift.

Intermediate leg position.

Advanced position.

Why must pregnant and postpartum women relearn how to get up and down correctly? Because the seated and back-lying transverse abdominal exercises do not work unless you get up and down correctly from the following positions. They don't work because it is impossible to hold the transverse in at the fifth floor in certain positions. And if you can't hold it in, the transverse goes forward forcefully against that weakened recti muscle, increasing the abdominal separation.

Going from a Seated to a Back-Lying Position. The correct way to do this is to hold the transverse in at the fifth floor, using your arms to lower yourself onto the floor from a side-lying position. Once your head touches the floor you can roll onto your back.

The incorrect way is to roll straight back, because you can't hold your transverse in.

Going from a Seated to
a Back-Lying Position.

① ② ③ ④ ⑤

Correct method.

Incorrect method.

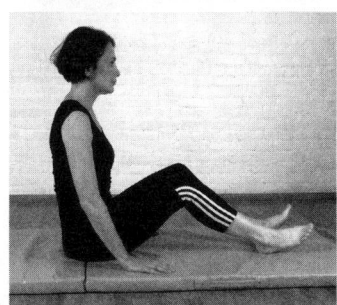

Correct method.

Sitting Up from a Back-Lying Position. The correct way to do this is to hold the transverse in at the fifth floor. Without lifting your head, roll your body like a log to the side. Continue to hold the transverse in as you use your arms to push yourself up to a sitting position.

The incorrect way is to bolt straight up. This is called a jackknife. Doing a jackknife puts a tremendous strain on the abdominals and makes it impossible to hold the transverse in. One jackknife can undo three weeks of transverse exercises. Why erase all the hard work you've done just to save a few seconds?

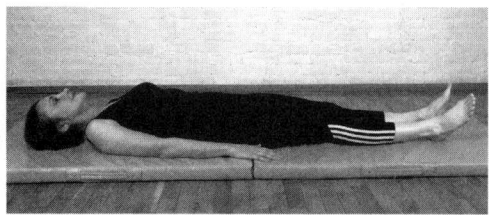

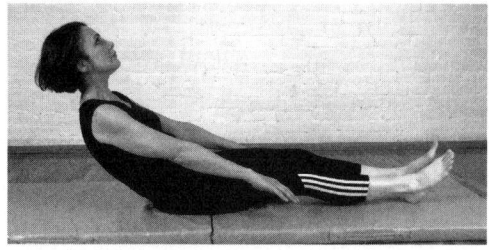

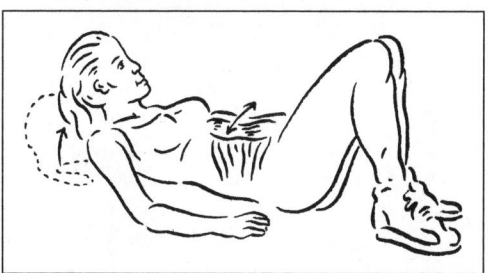

Incorrect method.

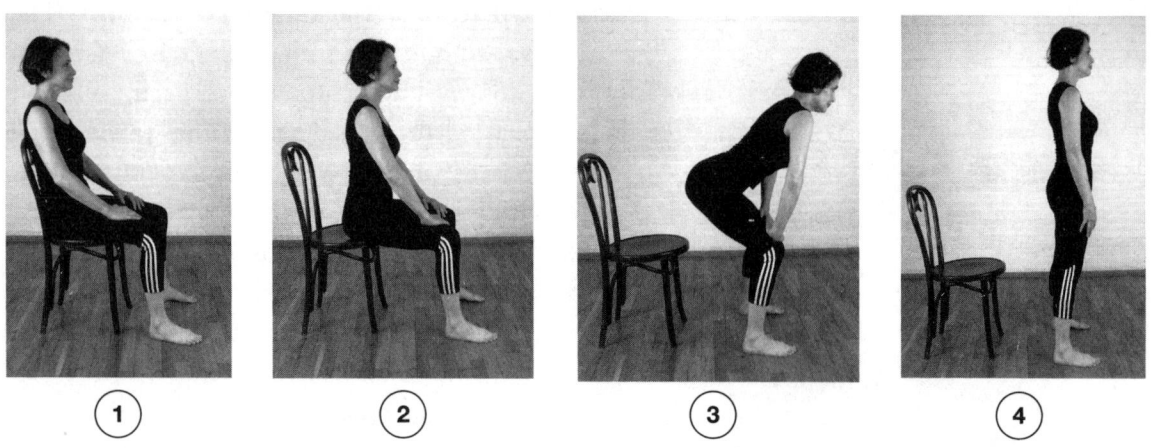

1   2   3   4

Getting Up from a Chair. Hold your transverse in as you scoot your butt to the edge of the chair. Put your hands on your thighs. Continue to hold your transverse in and bring yourself to the hands–above–knees position. Go to a standing position, keeping your back flat. You should sit down in a chair the same way you get up from one!

Going from a Seated to a Standing Position. Hold the transverse at the fifth floor and move onto all-fours. You can do a pelvic tilt while you are there! Now bring one leg way out in front of you so your foot is forward of your knee. Put your hands on the thigh of your forward leg to support your lower back. Continue to hold the transverse in as you come to a standing position. If you come straight up from a seated position, it is very hard on your knees because they are forward of your ankle bone. This forward position puts a lot of strain on your knees, which may still have some relaxin in them. You should reverse these positions when getting yourself to a seated position on the floor.

1   2   3   4

Kegels

Kegel exercises were developed by Arnold Kegel, MD, an American OB-GYN who worked with women with bladder-control problems. He saw how pregnancy and childbirth weaken and stretch out the pelvic floor muscles, and devised an exercise to treat the condition. Pregnancy weakens the pelvic floor muscles because, in her ninth month, a woman has an average of thirteen pounds weighing on her pelvic floor muscles. Strengthening these muscles not only keeps you from peeing in your pants when you cough, laugh, or jump (yup, it happens to the best of us), it will also enhance sexual pleasure and help keep those muscles strong as you age.

As I mentioned earlier, you can visualize your pelvic floor by thinking of your pelvis as a brown paper bag and your pelvic floor as the bottom of the bag. Your organs are your groceries. When the bottom of the bag gets wet (or weak), all your groceries will fall out (organ prolapse). Weak pelvic floor muscles also allow urine to leak out when you sneeze or cough. The first step to strengthening the pelvic floor muscles is to isolate them by being aware of how they work. I realize this is easier said than done for many women, especially after childbirth, when the muscles have been stretched out.

The main muscle of the pelvic floor is called the pubococcygeus, or the PC muscle.

A good way to identity your pelvic floor muscles is to pretend you are trying to stop the flow of your urine midstream. Many books will tell you to do this while you are actually urinating. Wrong, wrong, wrong! It's okay to locate the muscle this way, but never do Kegel exercises while you're urinating because it can promote a urinary tract infection, especially during pregnancy.

Also, remember to breathe while engaging these muscles. Holding your breath increases abdominal pressure and may stretch and weaken your pelvic floor muscles as well as make the diastasis larger. One way to keep from holding your breath is to count out loud as you are doing the exercises. Once you have identified the pelvic floor muscles and can engage them correctly without holding your breath, you are ready to begin my BAKS Kegel exercises.

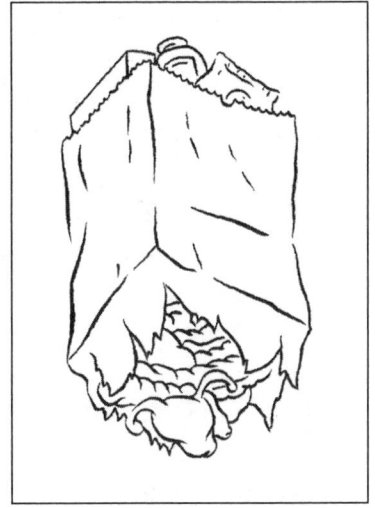

If you don't do your Kegels, your pelvic floor will become a pelvic basement.

Start by sitting in a chair with your legs apart. If you sit cross-legged or with your legs close together you will tend to use the muscles in your butt, and that does nothing much to help your PC muscle. Like my transverse exercises, you are going to imagine the muscle as an elevator, only this time it will go up and down, not sideways.

As you get stronger you will find it easier to do Kegels while you're standing or squatting. Try to get in as many Kegels as you can during the course of the day (while you're watching TV, feeding the baby, in the car, waiting on line at the supermarket, etc.). No one will know you're doing them but you!

Kegels I: The Ten-Second Hold.   Sit comfortably with your legs apart and your back supported against a wall or a chair. Bring your transverse to the fifth floor and hold it there as you engage your pelvic floor muscles. Pretend you are stopping the flow of urine. Hold both the PC muscle and the transverse muscle as tight as you can while you count to ten. Then relax both muscles. A good way to relax the pelvic floor muscle is to imagine it opening up like a flower. After each ten-second hold, do 10 quick squeeze/releases. Try to work up to doing 20 of these ten-second holds and squeeze/releases five times a day. That's one hundred PC holds and one hundred squeeze releases daily.

Starter's tip: If you're having difficulty holding in your PC for ten seconds at a time, start with a five-second hold, or do the Kegel exercise with your legs up on the wall (as you will do in later stretching exercises).

Kegels II: Elevators.   Sit comfortably with your legs apart and your back supported. Hold your transverse muscle at the fifth floor as you imagine that you are trying to pick up a penny using your vaginal lips. I know it's an odd image, but it works.

Think of an elevator that travels between five floors, the bellybutton being the fifth floor and the vaginal opening being the first floor. Bring the penny up from the first floor and take it through the second, third, and fourth toward the fifth floor. Hold the penny at the fifth floor and count to five. Make sure you are holding your transverse in at the fifth floor throughout the exercise.

Slowly bring the penny back down through the fourth, third, and second floors to the first floor. Now imagine your vagina opening up like a flower, and let the penny go. Then hold the muscle in again. After each elevator you need to do 10 quick squeeze/releases. Do 10 elevators, then 10 squeeze/releases, at least five times day.

Starter's tip: If the downward movement is difficult for you and your elevator crashes to the basement as you're counting down, don't worry. As the muscle gets stronger, the downward movement will be easier to control.

Squatting

I teach squatting exercises to pregnant women because a squat is the ideal position from which to give birth (not lying on your back, legs akimbo, as many of us are instructed in the hospital). For new moms, squatting strengthens the oblique abdominal muscles and the knees, and stretches the lower back, calves, and pelvic floor muscles.

Squatting also helps when going to the bathroom, because the squatting position supports and aligns the bowel to produce an easier and more complete evacuation. (The inventor of the toilet didn't know much about anatomy.) This will help if you are constipated, have hemorrhoids, or if you find going to the bathroom painful. Try using a small footstool (about seven inches high) to elevate your feet during bowel movements. You can also use a small square wastebasket. Just turn it on its side and put your feet on it. I also use an apparatus called a Welles Step, which fits around my toilet and does not take up any otherwise unused space. When I need it, I pull it out and put my feet on it, which puts me in a squatting position. When I am finished using it, it slides back around my toilet. You can view and purchase the Welles Step on my Web site, www.maternalfitness.com.

Squatting is a wonderful exercise in general. It's a natural position, although people in Western countries rarely use it. Just watch preschool children, who squat easily and all the time. Later, they begin to sit in chairs for prolonged periods like the rest of us. As a result, our calf muscles tighten and the joints of our ankles and backs become stiff. We should all re-experience the pleasure of squatting!

Squatting should not be hard on your knees—not if you get down and stay down for a while and bear your weight on the outsides of your feet. It's getting up from the squat that can put pressure on your knees. If you have knee problems, pain in your pubic area, or varicose veins in your vagina, consult your doctor before doing these exercises.

Note: Immediately after giving birth you might just want to squat while going to the bathroom instead of doing squatting exercises.

Squatting Exercise I. Stand with your feet flat and hip-distance apart. Hold on to an immovable object like a railing, doorjamb, or secured chair, and descend gradually, without bouncing, into a squat, bending your knees and making sure your heels are on the floor. With your feet pointing straight ahead, shift your weight to the outsides of your feet, keeping your arms

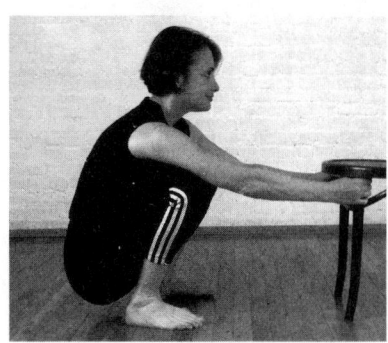

Make sure you hold onto an immovable object when squatting.

straight and at shoulder height, your knees lined up with your ankles and your head up.

Hold the squat. Work up to holding the position for a full minute at a time. Then gradually work your way up to five minutes at a time, several times a day. Remember to hold your transverse in! You can also do a Kegel while you're here.

Do not stand up from this position. This is very hard on your knees. Get out of the squat by lowering yourself to a sitting position one hand at a time. Before moving to a standing position, get onto all-fours and then into a hands-above-knees position.

Starter's tips: If you have trouble keeping your heels on the floor, try straightening your arms and pulling farther away from the object you are holding on to. If that doesn't work, try putting a rolled-up towel under your heels, wearing low heels, or sitting on a short stack of books.

You might find that your legs go to sleep at first, but your circulation will improve as you continue practicing your squats.

Stretching

If you have a cat, watch the next time it leans into a stretch. Notice how its back arches way up, then way down so that its belly is almost dragging on the floor. Its front legs and chest go way out, then its back legs and butt go way out. No wonder they have that look of sheer contentment afterwards!

Stretching is nature's prescription for relaxing the body. Most of us don't do it enough. Not only does it relieve stress, it helps keep you flexible where you want to be flexible. It's also a great way to lengthen those muscles that are shortened by carrying around a baby and pushing a stroller.

You've done some stretching work already with pelvic tilts and squatting (see pictures 1–3), both of which gently stretch out the muscles in your lower back. Now we're going to add three exercises that will stretch the muscles in your chest (those pectorals that shorten as your shoulders and neck come forward when taking care of the baby), as well as in your inner thighs and the backs of your legs.

Before you begin, keep in mind that there is a correct and incorrect way to stretch. The incorrect way is to stretch your muscle as far as it can go or to do quick, repetitive, bouncing movements like football players used to do when warming up, before we knew better. This is called ballistic stretching. It's harmful for the body and I go ballistic when I see someone doing it! When you do this, your muscles reflexively contract and get shorter instead of longer; this increases your chances of tearing muscle fibers. **Never bounce and never stretch beyond the point at which you feel discomfort.**

The correct way to stretch is called static stretching, which involves a slow, deliberate stretch through the muscle's full range of movement until you feel a tightness or resistance in the muscle. Stop before you feel pain. Hold the stretch for up to thirty seconds and then relax.

I love the idea of putting your mind in your muscle. Develop the habit of mentally focusing on the muscles you're working. This way, you'll do the exercises more efficiently. As you do these stretches, close your eyes and visualize the muscle. First, take a moment or two to "see" the muscle relaxing (tense muscles are in the shortened position), then imagine it lengthening as you breathe through the stretch.

Stretching I: Chest Muscles (Pectoral Stretch). Sit in a chair or on the floor with your back straight. Hold on to the ends of a belt, a small towel, or anything that is not elastic, and bring the object behind your head. Keep your elbows below your shoulders. Gently bring your elbows back behind your shoulders without arching your back.

Hold the stretch for thirty seconds. Relax. Do at least ten chest stretches a day.

Starter's tips: You'll probably feel some tension in your upper arm muscles. Keep your arms

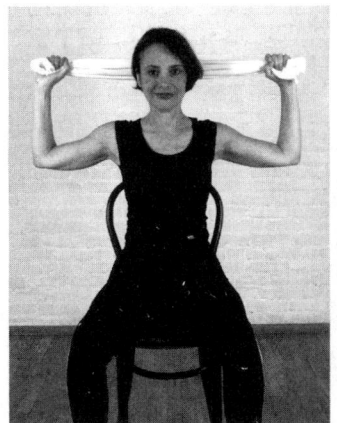 

You can do a chest muscle stretch either on a chair or on the floor.

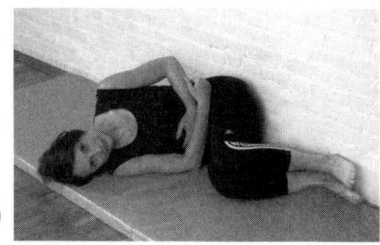

(1)

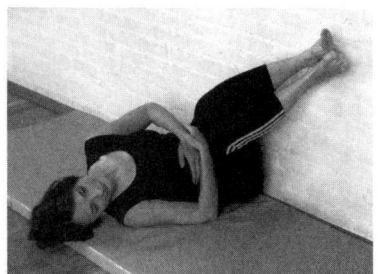

(2)

(3)

(4)

Getting into the inner thigh wall stretch correctly.

relaxed and focus on lengthening those chest muscles. Don't bend your wrists or arch your back. This stretch is great for moms who spend a lot of time behind a desk.

Stretching II: Inner Thighs. Using your arms from a sitting position on the floor, hold your transverse at the fifth floor as you lower yourself to your side. Put your butt against the wall. Your body should now be in an L-position. Keeping your head on the floor, roll onto your back. With bent knees and transverse in, slowly walk your legs up the wall. Now, slowly separate your legs into a V-shape until you feel a stretch along your inner thighs. Hold the stretch for thirty seconds, then relax. If you like, you can do some Kegels while you're relaxing. Remember to engage the abdominals at the same time.

Hold your transverse in at the fifth floor as you bring your legs together. Then walk your feet down the wall to your side to get out of this position. This is important because if you take your feet off the wall to get down, you cannot hold your transverse in. Once your feet are on the floor and you are in a side-lying position, hold your transverse in and bring yourself to a sitting position with your arms. Do at least one thirty-second stretch each day. Work up to 3 thirty-second stretches a day.

Starter's tips: You can put a pillow under your head if this feels more comfortable. If you are very flexible and your legs flop open when you get them up against the wall, this isn't a good exercise for you. Skip it. To prevent injury

(1)

(2)

(3)

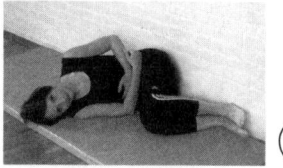

(4)

Getting out of the stretch correctly.

to your joints, it's important not to overstretch. It's a good idea to do this exercise in the morning. However, doing inner thigh stretches after you've been on your feet all day can help reduce swelling in your legs.

Stretching III: Backs of Legs.   Sit on the floor with one leg straight in front of you, foot lined up with the thigh, and with your other leg bent at the knee, foot resting against the knee of the straight leg. Put a splint or a piece of fabric the length of a scarf around your foot and hold the ends in your hands, wrapping it around your hands once so the fabric is taut.

Sit up straight with your shoulders lined up with your hips. Close your eyes, relax your straightened knee, and imagine the muscles down the back of your leg relaxing. Now pull the splint. You should feel a stretch in your calf area. Sit up straight and stick out your buttocks. You should now feel a stretch along the back of your entire leg.

Close your eyes and breathe through the stretch. Expand your belly and bring your transverse toward your spine as you exhale. Feel those muscles releasing, relaxing, and lengthening like Jell-O. Hold the stretch for twenty to thirty seconds. Repeat with the other leg. Do at least 1 twenty- to thirty-second stretch once a day. This is also a great stretch to do after an aerobic exercise.

Starter's tips: Remember to keep the transverse in while stretching. Also, keep your feet in a flexed position; you will feel the stretch more in this position. You can also do this stretch sitting in a chair. Do not round your back.

You can do the leg stretch on the floor or in a chair.

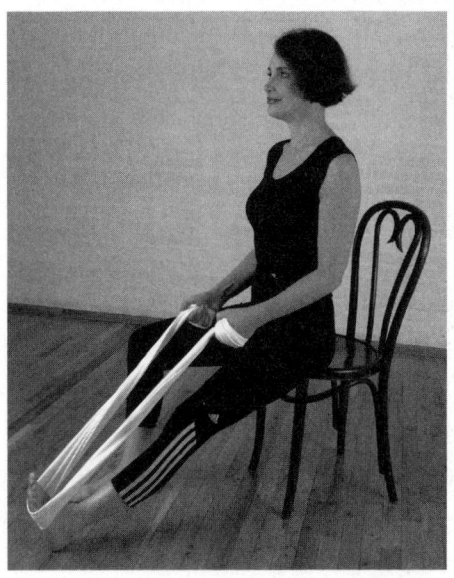

Strengthening

Now that you have become familiar with the stretching movements in the BAKS Basics, I want to be sure you understand the connection between *stretching* muscles and *strengthening* them.

You want to strengthen the muscles that are getting longer and weaker because of the postural changes that come from carrying and feeding the baby and the joint laxity that comes from the relaxin that stays in your body after pregnancy.

The BAKS Basics exercises strengthen your abdominals with the Tupler Technique and the muscles of your pelvic floor with Kegels. Exercises for your upper back (another important area for a new mom to strengthen) will be included in the fifteen- and thirty-minute workouts. Strong muscles can lift, carry, hold, push, pull, and do whatever work is necessary when caring for an infant or small child. In doing the BAKS Basics and the Tupler Workouts (which I will cover later), you are working to contract and shorten those muscles that need to be strong—the muscles you need to do the work of carrying and lifting. Of course, you will be engaging your transverse muscle during every exercise.

At the same time, your muscles must be flexible—that is, stretchy. Muscles that are too tight cannot move your limbs in a coordinated and controlled manner. A muscle that is both strong and flexible is a toned muscle, capable of doing work, pulling your bones together, and enabling your body to move efficiently and smoothly.

This balance between strengthening and stretching the muscles is central to all of my postpartum exercise routines. If you follow my instructions, you will not be in danger of stressing ligaments, grinding joints, or fraying tendons. Ouch! You will be developing toned muscles, which will help you to regain your pre-pregnancy figure, or to have a body even better than you had before.

We've just covered the BAKS Basics. Make them a part of your life the first few weeks after giving birth so you can build up to the full fifteen- and thirty-minute Tupler Workouts. Once you have the belly breathing down pat, and you can keep your abdominals in at the fifth floor, you'll be ready to breathe correctly through the workout. Your lower back will start to feel better and you'll find that you have better control of your body.

Remember that you don't have to go through the entire BAKS routine in one fell swoop. Everyone's recovery is different. Do as much as you can. Just doing your Kegels or Tupler Technique abdominal exercises throughout the day might be enough to start. You can follow the sequence as I've presented it here, or you can make up your own routine. You can also do targeted exercises for your feet, wrists, and knees (see Chapter 4), or any body part that is causing you pain or discomfort. Whatever you do is better than doing nothing at all!

The Fifteen-Minute Tupler Workout

The golden rule for postpartum exercising is to start early and increase gradually. It's important to get started with the abdominals and pelvic floor right away, so begin with the BAKS Basics. Not only will this help with your recovery, but it will make you feel good about doing something positive for yourself. Although most active women return to exercise soon after delivery, they don't reach their pre-delivery performance level for at least two to three months. It usually takes around six months to feel like you did before you were pregnant. For you Type A's out there, have patience and don't try to do too much too soon. By week two, you will be ready to start some weight-bearing exercises, increasing gradually with time.

You can start by doing my fifteen-minute workout below three times a week, then move up to five days when you're up to it. When you're ready, you can move up to the thirty-minute workout. Remember to do your Kegels while you are resting between sets.

1. Neck Stretch (one minute)

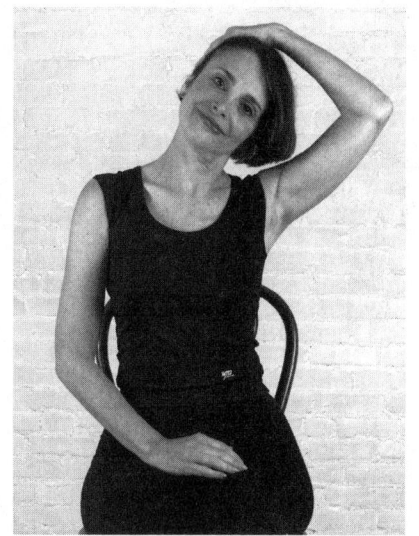

Sitting in a chair or on the floor, straighten your neck and drop your chin gently. Hold this position as you take your right hand and place it on the left side of your head above the temple. Gently bring your right ear toward your right shoulder, using your hand as a weight to stretch the left side of your neck. Close your eyes and slowly move your left shoulder toward the floor. Do this for thirty seconds on each side by counting very slowly to thirty.

Starter's tip: Make sure you do not jut out your chin as you are doing these exercises. Keep your shoulders relaxed.

2. Shoulder Circles (fifteen seconds)

You can do this exercise while sitting in the chair. Roll your shoulders back in full circles 8 times. Don't roll forward because new moms tend to round their shoulders forward when holding, feeding, or changing the baby.

3. Crossover Arm Stretches (one minute)

Take one arm straight across your chest, holding onto the wrist with the other hand. Now relax both shoulders. Turn your head toward the shoulder you are stretching. Close your eyes and gently move the shoulder you are now facing toward the floor. Hold for thirty seconds and repeat on the other side. You should feel this stretch behind your shoulder.

4. Chest Stretch/Upper Back Strengthening (one minute)

Sitting straight up in your chair, hold your resistance band in both hands, grabbing about an inch in your fists on each side. (The shorter you make the band, the more difficult the exercise.) Place the band on your chest above your breasts, keeping your wrists flat. Take a belly breath and pull your transverse muscle to the fifth floor; continue to hold it at the fifth floor as you straighten your arms out to the side so your shoulders are lined up with your wrists. Keep your elbows straight but soft and your shoulders down and relaxed. Think about energy flowing down your arms and out of your knuckles. While holding this position, do 30 contractions with your abs from the fifth to the sixth floor. (At the sixth floor, you're imagining that your bellybutton is pushing out beyond the back of your spine.) Count out loud to 30. Rest for a moment and then do another set. You can also do this in a seated position on the floor.

You can do the chest stretch on a chair or on the floor.

Starter's tip: Make sure you don't arch your back. In this exercise, your chest is getting longer and your upper back muscles are getting shorter.

5. Seated Transverse
(two minutes, thirty seconds)

Sit up straight in your chair, placing one hand under your breasts and one on your bellybutton. Take a belly breath and expand your belly. Now bring your bellybutton from the first floor to the fourth floor. This is your starting position. (I am assuming you have been doing the transverse exercises and are now ready to progress to the fourth floor.) Now bring your bellybutton to the fifth floor. As it goes back toward your spine, imagine your ribs coming together. Squeeze and hold it a moment at the fifth floor as you count out loud. Then release to the fourth floor before starting the next repetition. Do 100 squeeze-and-holds. If you're counting out loud, I know you're breathing! You should feel this exercise in your back and your abdominals. End each set with a belly breath, bringing your bellybutton all the way back toward your spine once more as you exhale. One set is 100 contractions. It takes two-and-a-half minutes. You should be doing a minimum of five sets of 100 daily.

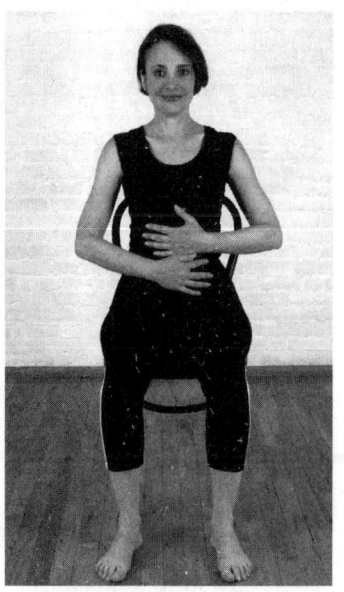

Hand position for seated transverse exercises.

If you get out of breath while doing this exercise, slow down and count out loud with more volume in your voice. Use a splint when you start doing the exercise from the fifth to the sixth floor.

6. Abdominal/Transverse Exercise on All-Fours *(fifteen seconds)*

Get down on all-fours, palms flat on the floor, knees hip-distance apart, toes touching the floor. Keeping your back flat and still, bring your transverse to the third floor. This is your starting position. Now bring your bellybutton toward your spine at the fifth floor. Squeeze and hold it there a moment, then release to the third floor before you start the next repetition. Count out loud as you do 15 contractions from the third to the fifth floor.

Starting position for transverse exercise on all fours.

7. Standing Hip Flexor Stretch (one minute)

Hip flexor stretch.

This exercise is sometimes called the runner's stretch. Stand with one leg in front of the other, hip-distance apart, with the back leg straight and the front leg bent. The distance between your legs should be about eighteen inches. Make sure your knee is not forward of your ankle-bone. For balance, you may want to hold on to a wall or secured chair while doing this stretch. Keeping your back leg straight and your transverse in at the fifth floor, think of bringing your pubic bone toward your navel. Hold it there for a count of fifteen. Now do the other leg. You should feel this stretch at the top of your leg. My hand in the photo is on the hip flexor, which is where you should feel this stretch.

8. Back of Leg Stretch (one minute)

Back of leg stretch.

Sit on the edge of your chair with one leg bent and one leg straight, with your hands on the thigh of your bent leg. Flex the foot of the straight leg (toes toward the ceiling), keeping the back of your leg straight. Lean forward with a flat back, keeping your hands on the thigh of your bent leg. Go as far as you can until you feel the stretch. Stick out your butt to get even more of a stretch. Do not stick out your chin. Keep your shoulders relaxed. Hold for fifteen seconds and repeat on the other side. You can also do this stretch standing up.

9. Inner Thigh Stretch (thirty seconds)

Sit up straight on the edge of your chair (a sturdy one with no wheels) with your legs straight, your feet flexed, and your thighs apart in a V. (As with the previous inner thigh stretch, don't do this exercise if you have a pain in your pubic bone.) Put your fists on the seat of the chair behind you, near your butt. Stick your butt and chest out for an easy inner thigh stretch. Do not round your upper back as you come forward to get a stretch. Instead, bend over at your hips. Hold the stretch for thirty seconds. Do not hold your breath. Remember to count out loud. This stretch can also be done on the floor, in a seated or a back-lying position.

10. Headlifts (one minute)

It is difficult to work in a back-lying position because gravity makes it harder to engage the transverse muscle in this position. This is why it's important to strengthen your transverse muscle whenever you feed the baby in a seated position, where gravity makes it easier. You should be doing at least 500 seated transverse exercises per day for at least two weeks before you start these headlifts.

Begin on your back with a belly breath so your muscles are at the first floor when you start the exercise and in on the work of lifting your head. When you lift your head and shoulders off the

floor, it is impossible to engage your transverse muscle. And if you can't hold in your transverse, you are increasing your diastasis. So instead of making the exercise harder by lifting your head higher, you can make it harder by bringing your heels farther away from your buttocks. The farther away your heels are from your butt, the higher the small of your back comes off the floor. The higher your back comes off the floor, the harder it is to use your abdominals to put it on the floor during the exercise. Remember that promise

Starting position for headlift.

Ending position.

you made to me at the beginning of the book? Only your head comes off the floor. No shoulders!

Do not jut your chin out when lifting your head. To prevent this, press the back of your neck on the floor before lifting your head. When you jut you cannot hold your transverse in. Lift your head by saying "yes." Remember, this is not a crunch or sit-up—it is a headlift. Put your splint around your abdominal separation to hold the two halves of your abdominal muscles together. (If you have a separation at the top, splint at the top under the ribs; if your separation is in the middle, splint in the middle; and so on.) If you have a diastasis in all three places, do one set in each position, starting with where it is the worst (usually in the middle, at the bellybutton or just above it).

Lying on your back, with the splint underneath you, take your left hand and grab the splint on the right side, pulling it toward the middle. Do the same with the other hand on the other side, ending with both hands resting together on your bellybutton or just above it. Relax your arms on the floor.

With knees bent and feet close to your buttocks, do these four steps:

a. Take a belly breath to expand your belly to the first floor. Bring your transverse to the fifth floor (toward your spine). As your belly moves back toward your spine, imagine your ribs coming together. Do not use your pelvis when bringing your transverse to your spine.

b. Hold your transverse at the fifth floor as you think of your bellybutton zipping up under your ribs. This puts the small of your back on the floor.

c. Think of pulling your ribs together as you pull the splint towards the middle of your body. Continue to hold the splint after you've pulled it together.

d. Press the back of your neck on the floor, contract your transverse muscle from the fifth to the sixth floor as you lift your head, bringing your chin to your chest, and count out loud. Hold your transverse at the fifth floor as you put your head back down on the floor.

Do one set of 10 headlifts.

11. Seated Military Press (one minute)

Sit on a chair or on the floor with a resistance band under your buttocks. Hold the ends of your band in your hands (the more band you hold in your fists, the harder the exercise). Start with your elbows down by your sides, wrists flat, shoulders lined up with your hips. Take a belly breath and bring your transverse into the fifth-floor position. Now contract to the sixth floor as you straighten your arms directly up toward the ceiling without touching your hands together. Keep the transverse at the fifth floor as you slowly bring your arms back down to the starting position. Count out loud as you do

Starting position for seated military press.

Correct ending position.

Incorrect ending position.

Starting position in chair.

two sets of 12 repetitions. Think of your abs doing the work of lifting your arms—this makes it much easier to work the abdominals and arms at the same time!

Straighten your arms as much as you can without locking your elbows, using slow, controlled movements. Do not arch your back.

Note: If you have shoulder problems, lifting your arms overhead with either a resistance band or weights is not a good idea.

Starter's tips: The number of repetitions is not as important as the quality of each movement. If you feel pain, stop and rest before trying to resume the exercise. If the muscle you're contracting feels tired, stop the repetitions even if you have not performed the designated number. Do not bring your hands together while doing this exercise. In this exercise as well as the other resistance band exercises, to make the exercise harder, make the band shorter by putting more of it in your hands. Eventually, when it gets too short, you will need to get a higher-resistance band. The next level is purple.

12. Rowing (one minute)

Sit on the front of a sturdy chair. Put your band under your feet, grabbing the ends with your fingernails, palms facing each other. Your shoulders should be lined up with your elbows and hips; your knees should be bent. Hold your transverse at the fifth floor and then move to the sixth floor as you bring your elbows back. Stay at the fifth floor as you bring your arms back to the starting position. Your elbows should not be forward of your shoulders, as this rounds the shoulders.

Again, do this using slow, controlled movements. Count out loud on the backward movement to make sure that you are breathing. Do two sets of 12 repetitions.

Starting position for rowing.

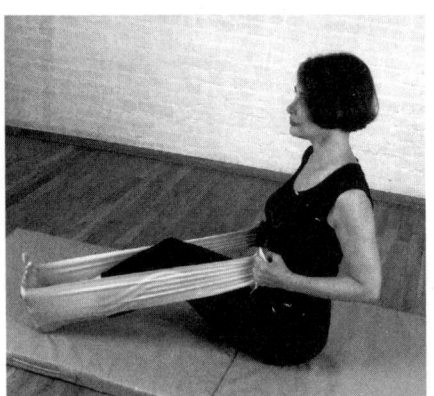
Ending position.

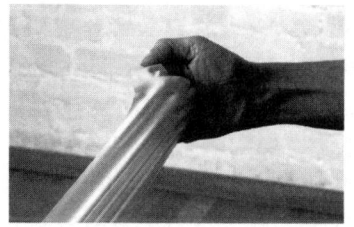

Starter's tip: With this exercise, digging your fingernails into the band helps to keep your wrists straight (see photo at left). Don't use your wrists to pull the band. Your whole forearm should move as one unit. This exercise can also be done sitting on the floor.

13. Chest Press (one minute)

Put your resistance band on your back and under your armpits, holding the ends of the band in your fists with your arms in an L-position. Take a belly breath and bring your transverse to the fifth floor. It stays at the fifth floor for the whole exercise. Slowly straighten your arms out in front of you as if you are punching someone with both fists. Count out loud as you do two sets of 12. Remember to keep your chest wide, shoulders down, relaxed wrists flat, and back straight. Do not bring your arms together on the forward movement, as this rounds the shoulders. Remember, the shorter the band, the more resistance and the harder the exercise.

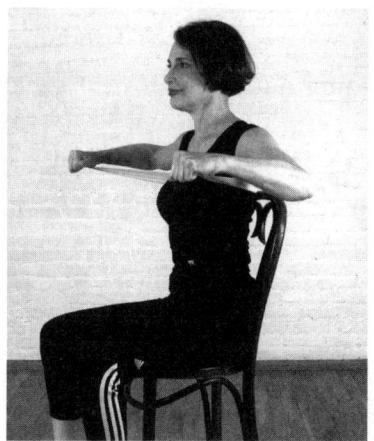

Starting position for chest press.

Ending position.

Incorrect ending position.

Starting position for
wall squat without splint.

Ending position.

Wall squat with splint.

Wall squat with ball.

14. Squat Holds Against the Wall (one minute)

This exercise can be done with or without a splint. Place your back against the wall with your feet way out ahead of you. (You can also do this exercise with a stabilization ball between your back and the wall.) Now slide your back down the wall until your knees are lined up with your buttocks, holding your transverse at the fifth floor. If this position is too hard for you because your legs are not strong enough, do not go down so far. Make sure your knees are always directly lined up with your ankles and not in front of them.

Then imagine your bellybutton going out through your back to the sixth floor as you slide up the wall. Hold it at the fifth floor as you come back down the wall. Do 2 sets of 20 of these up-and-down squats. You will really feel this exercise in your legs.

15. Outer Thigh Exercise with Resistance Band (thirty seconds)

Note: Don't do this exercise if you have pubic pain.

Sit back in your sturdy chair, putting the resistance band around your flexed feet. Hold on to the band with each hand, fingernails gripping the ends. Sit up straight, elbows lined up with your shoulders, shoulders lined up with hips, and take a belly breath,

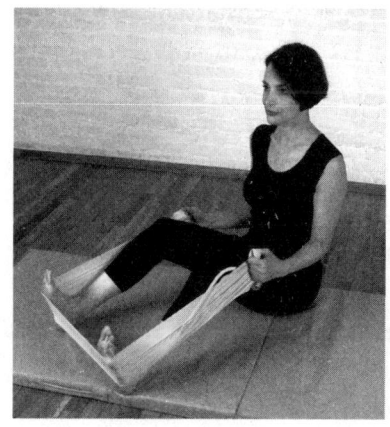

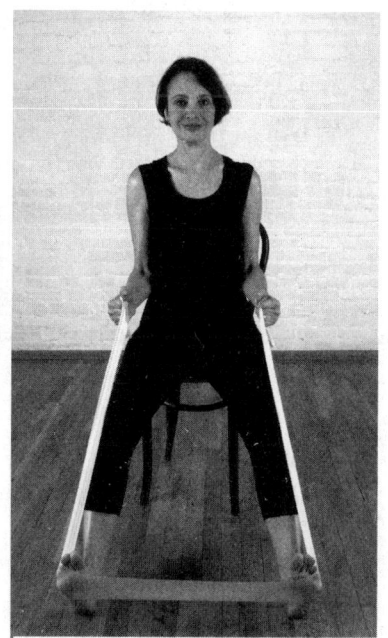

pulling your transverse in to the fifth floor. Hold it there as you move your right leg out to the side until you feel it in your outer thigh. Move your left leg out to the side until you feel it in your outer thigh. Hold this position. Count out loud as you do two sets of 15 transverse contractions from the fifth to the sixth floor. This exercise can also be done in a seated position on the floor. Do the Kegel exercise between each set.

16. Inner Thigh Press (thirty seconds)

Sit on the floor with your knees bent. Bend forward with a straight back, putting your elbows between your knees and your hands in a prayer position. Hold your transverse at the fifth floor. Now contract your belly from the fifth to the sixth floor as you bring your knees in toward each other using your elbows as resistance. Make sure your shoulders stay down and relaxed. Count out loud as you do two sets of 10 repetitions. Do the Kegel exercise between each set.

17. Back Stretch with Breathing/Relaxation (thirty seconds)

From a side-lying position, hold your transverse at the fifth floor and use your arms to lower yourself to the floor. Remember, your head should touch the floor before you roll onto your back. Put your arms on the floor by your sides and bend your knees, bringing your heels close to your buttocks. Hold your transverse at the fifth floor, keeping your feet on the floor, and roll your knees to one side. Look over your opposite shoulder.

Close your eyes and breathe through this stretch. Expand your belly and exhale as you visualize the muscles in your neck, shoulders, and back releasing and your entire body relaxing and lengthening like Jell-O. Take about fifteen breaths. Hold your transverse in at the fifth floor, keeping your feet on the floor, as you roll your knees to the opposite side, looking over your other shoulder. Continue to breathe into the stretch with another fifteen breaths. If you bring your heels away from your buttocks while you are doing this stretch, you will feel it more in your upper back.

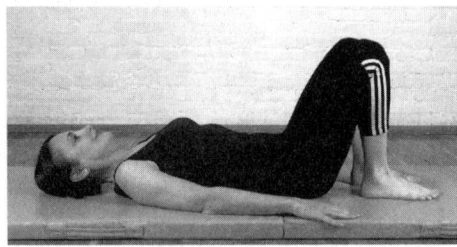

Starting position for lower back stretch.

Ending position.

Starting position for upper back stretch.

Ending position.

3

Using the Tupler Technique When Recovering from C-Sections, Episiotomies, and Other Physical Traumas

Cesareans

DID YOU KNOW that cesarean sections (commonly called C-sections) were named after the Roman emperor Caesar, who was reportedly born through a cut in his mother's abdominal or uterine wall? The cesarean delivery rate declined during the late 1980s through the mid–1990s but has been on the rise since 1996, according to the International Cesarean Awareness Network. Although there has been controversy among the medical community about the frequent use of the procedure, more than one-fourth (26 percent) of all children born in the United States in 2002 were delivered by cesarean, the highest level ever reported in this country. The rate of vaginal births after a previous cesarean delivery has dropped 23 percent.

C-sections require longer stays in the hospital and longer recovery time than do vaginal deliveries. Just because you've had a C-section doesn't mean your pelvic floor muscles haven't been stretched out. This is a common misconception. Your pelvic floor muscles are weakened by the weight of the organs during the pregnancy, regardless of how you deliver.

If you have had a cesarean section, you will need extra care and attention after you leave the hospital. Your body must recover from major abdominal surgery as well from nine months of pregnancy. Everyone heals at a different speed, so don't let anyone else's recovery story make you feel badly. Listen to your body and respond to its needs. Most women who have had C-sections experience at least some of the following symptoms:

- Pain when coughing or sneezing
- Soreness around the incision
- Severe gas pains
- Difficulty getting out of bed
- Difficulty straightening up and reaching overhead
- A pulling sensation in the belly when standing up
- Pain when going to the bathroom
- Discomfort when nursing (from the baby's weight and movements)

I agree with Caroline C. Creager, author of *Bounce Back into Shape after Baby*, who wrote, "More often than not cesarean birth is downplayed in our society as minor surgery. As a physical therapist I routinely ask my clients, 'Have you had any type of surgery?' If the woman's response is, 'Yes, I had a cesarean section,' I would unconsciously categorize this as a minor type of surgery. My second child Michael was born by cesarean due to his breech position and cardiac problems. Now I know better than to assume just because cesarean births are common that this type of surgery is minor. I will never make that mistake again. In order for a child to be born by cesarean the obstetrician must cut through the skin, connective tissue, abdominal muscles, which are usually moved aside. The surgeon must then pull to get the baby out, causing additional soreness and bruising. No wonder you are very sore and have difficulty getting out of bed and walking!"

Recovering from a C-Section

Believe it or not, the best thing you can do to help speed recovery along is to move around as soon as possible, although you might want to take it easy for the first two days. During this time, ask someone to help you get out of bed and support you while you walk. Remember to bring your transverse to the fifth floor while you are doing this. Follow the RICE technique: Rest, Ice, Compress, and Elevate. Get yourself into a comfortable position. Apply cold ice packs to the injured area for brief, regular periods.

Quickly and gently apply moderate pressure over the area. Elevate your feet, legs, and bottom with pillows. Your feet should be above your heart.

After that, walking around will help prevent fluid from settling in your lungs and producing a respiratory infection. It also gets your blood circulating (never a bad thing in recovery), reduces swelling in the area of the incision, strengthens the muscles, and helps the digestive process. I also suggest that you do my transverse exercises at this time. The gentle pumping action of the muscles helps promote healing by increasing circulation and reducing swelling in the area of the incision. If you are in severe pain or are bleeding, stop all exercising and consult your physician.

If you are thinking about having a second child, you might want to talk to your doctor about VBACs (vaginal births after cesareans). For more information about C-sections, go to www.acog.org and www.midwife.org.

Here are some other things you can do to speed along your recovery:

Coughing Exercise

Try to make yourself cough 5 times every half-hour. This not only clears your lungs, it also forces you to breathe in fresh air. Holding your transverse in while you cough will help reduce the pain by supporting your stomach. You can also take a pillow, sheet, or towel and press it firmly over the incision while you cough.

Huffing

If you did Lamaze breathing, you will have an idea about how to huff. Huffing is similar, but faster and louder. Bring your transverse to the fifth floor as you say "hut!" 5 times, fast and loud. You will feel your muscles contracting with each exhalation. Do this every half-hour.

TENS Units

Transcutaneous Electrical Nerve Stimulations (TENS) have been used with great success on women who have had C-sections and want to reduce their medication and get out of bed faster. They are portable, easy-to-use devices that give a constant, non-painful stimulus to the abdominal muscles, which blocks the pain. They also help reduce gas pains and flatulence.

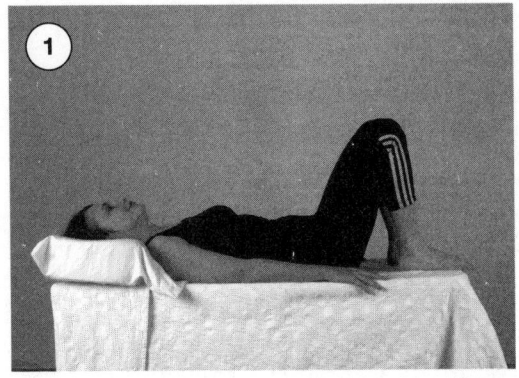

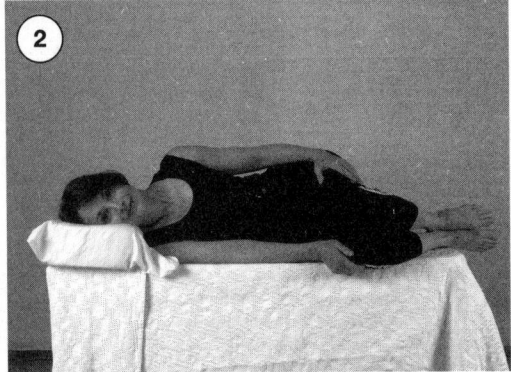

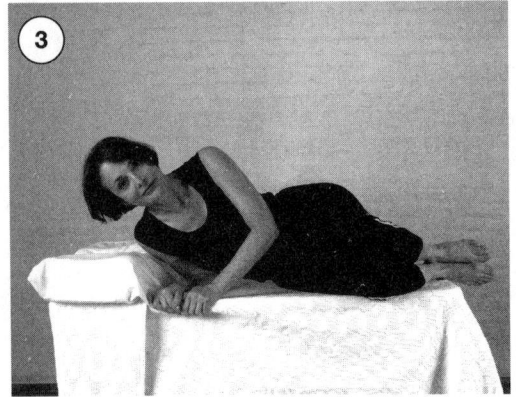

Getting In and Out of Bed

Take extra care getting out of bed by "log rolling" so you don't put pressure on your abdominal incisions and back (think of your body as a log). Lie on your back. Hold your transverse at the fifth floor and bend your knees by drawing up one knee at a time. Without lifting your head, roll to your side, keeping your knees together. Place your elbows and other hand on the bed. Push up with your elbow and hand as you lower your feet off the bed. Keep pushing until you are in a sitting position. To get into bed, do the same thing in reverse.

Scar Massage

Exercises and scar-tissue massages that pull on this fragile scar tissue are not recommended for the first five to eight days after surgery. However, scar-tissue massages can and should be done after the incision has healed and the staples have been removed. This is important to prevent adhesions (scar tissue sticking to tissues beneath it).

Be gentle at first, and if you are feeling any pain, reduce the pressure. Massage the scar tissue by working it with a rubbing motion along the line of the scar. Stroke back and forth across the scar. Roll the scar between your thumb and your forefinger. The goal is to move the skin and the muscles underneath so that they appear to slide freely over one another.

For the best results, try massaging your scar two to three times a day for five to ten minutes. The more you massage the scar, the faster it will heal. Aside from the healing benefits, massaging your scar will help it become less visible with time. It is possible to see results in three to four weeks. If you feel itching or numbness around the incision site, it is because the nerves that were cut during the operation are beginning to regenerate. This nerve recovery will probably last for some time, while the scar tissue itself will be numb. You can read more about scar massage in *How to Raise Children without Breaking Your Back* by Alex Pirie and Hollis Herman, which is available on my Web site, www.maternalfitness.com.

(continued from page 48)

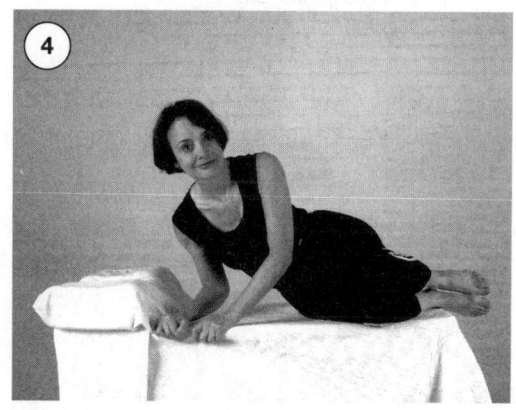

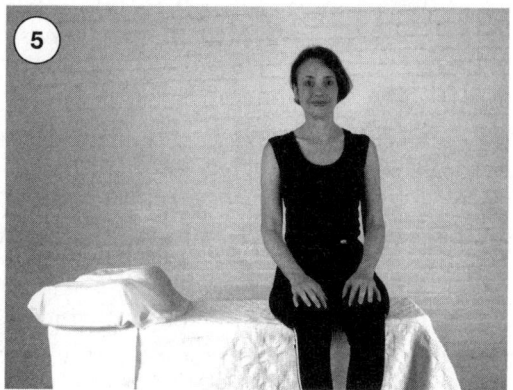

Scar Taping

If you have a sensitive scar and don't want to massage it, you might want to try taping, a new approach to reducing scar tissue. Placing stretchy Kinesiotape onto the scar will put gentle pressure on the scar as it is pulled off the muscle. This is important to prevent adhesions. Scar taping can be left on for twenty-four to forty-eight hours (until it falls off), and it will work while you sleep! To order the tape, call 1–800–523–0912.

Splinting After a C-Section

Many women ask me if it's okay to use a splint after C-sections. I advise them to wait until the scar is healed (approximately four to six weeks) before using the splint.

Hemorrhoids

Unfortunately, hemorrhoids, those stretched-out veins around the anus, are a common part of the aftermath of delivery, brought on by constipation or the strain of pushing during labor. As I mentioned in my section on chairs, you can buy a special hemorrhoid pillow to make sitting more comfortable, or you can use a breast-feeding pillow such as a Boppy or My Breast Friend. You can also use a Welles Step or footstool when you are on the toilet. The Welles Step helps support and align your bowel to make elimination easier. Taking a twenty- to thirty-minute hot sitz bath (a shallow bath taken in a seated position so that only the hips and buttocks are immersed in water) at least once a day will also help.

Remember to use your abdominal muscles (transverse at fifth floor) every time you have a bowel movement. As in delivery, when you push using your abdominal muscles, you will prevent the hemorrhoids from getting worse or coming back.

Episiotomies

In my opinion, episiotomies—surgical cuts in the perineum muscle (the area between the vagina and the rectum)—should be done only in emergency situations. Medical literature now supports the belief that there is no benefit to an episiotomy unless forceps are being used during delivery. That being said, seven out of every ten vaginal births in the United States involve episiotomies. The reason doctors cut is to prevent tearing, which is often jagged and difficult to sew up. Unfortunately, cutting can lead to further tearing during the birth, and recovering from an episiotomy can be more difficult for the mom than recovering from natural tearing. Additionally, the scar tissue that forms in the area can further weaken the muscles that are already stretched out after the pregnancy.

Tearing

Even if you did not have an episiotomy, you might have experienced a tear of the perineum during a vaginal delivery. Tearing in this area can be a minor skin laceration or, in extreme cases, can damage the perineal muscles in the anus, urethra, and even the clitoris and rectum. Like episiotomies, severe tears require stitches and cause a considerable amount of pain. Studies have found that pain in this region can last anywhere from two months to a year after childbirth.

Recovering from an Episiotomy or Tear

One thing you can do immediately is use ice packs to reduce the pain and swelling during the first few days. Ice packs can be applied every two hours, for seven to ten minutes at a time. Commercial ice packs that contain a flexible gel are the best because they conform to your body; these are available at most drug stores. You can also fill a rubber glove with ice chips or water, placing it on the bottom of a small bowl in the freezer to give it a rounded shape. Be careful not to put the packs directly on your bare skin. You should always have a layer of clothing or a cloth in between. Ice or cold packs applied directly to the skin for too long can freeze the tissue, and, since you may not have much feeling down there, you won't realize this is happening.

You might also want to get a squirt bottle filled with warm water to keep yourself clean after going to the bathroom (a painful proposition in itself), or, get a Therablue Spray that attaches easily to your sink. You can order this on my web site www.maternalfitness.com. Of course, sitting down will be painful, so you can use the hemorrhoid or nursing pillows I mentioned earlier.

Engaging your pelvic floor muscles (the ones you use doing the Kegels) by tightening whenever you sit down and get up will help decrease the pain in this area. Do this (along with the Tupler Technique) while you are feeding the baby as well. If you didn't do your Kegel exercises while you were pregnant, it will take a bit longer to feel those muscles again. Doing Kegel exercises twenty-four hours after birth will help circulate the blood in this area, which will accelerate the healing process (see Chapter 2). If you are not able to feel these muscles, don't get discouraged. Try doing Kegels while seated, standing, and lying down with your legs up on the wall, to see which way helps you feel the muscles tightening.

In most cases, there are no serious repercussions to having an episiotomy or tear, but sometimes a scar will stick to the muscles underneath, forming what's called an adhesion. Most women won't have adhesions from episiotomies or tears, but if you do you might have the following symptoms:

- Pain during intercourse
- Difficulty inserting a diaphragm or cervical cap
- Discomfort inserting a tampon
- Soreness between the vagina and rectum
- Discomfort having bowel movements

Adhesions can be prevented and treated by massaging the area. Massaging scars will reduce their size and rigidity, even in those that are ten or twenty years old, but the sooner you do this the better. Once the stitches have dissolved, you can begin to massage the tissues between your vagina and anus. Insert your thumb into the vagina while keeping your index finger over the perineal area above the scar. Gently roll the tissue between your thumb and finger. You can use a warm compress to relax the muscles and reduce any discomfort.

It's worth the initial discomfort because massaging your scar will make it become smaller, more elastic, and less tender. This allows the muscles to function without binding to one another. If they do bind together, you will experience pain during intercourse and the other symptoms I mentioned above. If this has happened to you, ask your doctor about ultrasound treatments (not the same ultrasound that was used to view your fetus), which will make the scarred area less painful to the touch and intercourse more pleasurable. You can read more about scar massage in *How to Raise Children without Breaking Your Back*.

Breast-Feeding Problems

If you are breast-feeding your baby, you will have a unique set of physical experiences that range from the painful to the sublime. When all goes well (and it doesn't always), nursing can be a joy for mom and baby alike. Here's what you can do to get over some of the common hurdles:

Breast Engorgement

Around the fourth day after the baby is born, your breasts might start looking like Macy's Thanksgiving balloons and feel like a quarry of rocks. This happens when production outpaces demand, and it can be painful. To make matters worse, the areola (the circle around the nipple) gets distended, making it harder for the baby to latch on, so she feeds less, causing more engorgement.

If your breasts are engorged, massage them in a warm shower or apply warm compresses before nursing. You can also pump or manually express milk until your breasts are back to their normal softness. Place your thumb on your breast, above the areola, and your fingers underneath. Gently but firmly roll and slide the thumb and fingers toward each other and onto the areola while compressing the breast tissue. You can also try the following to help ease the pain:

- If warm showers and compresses don't work, try using cold compresses as you express milk.

- Try different positions for feeding the baby (sitting up, lying down, etc.).

- Gently massage your breasts from under the arm and down the nipple. This will help reduce soreness and ease milk flow.

- Don't skip feedings. Make sure you nurse every two hours.

Stress and fatigue can also interfere with the release of the milk you're producing, so try doing some breathing and relaxation exercises. While your baby is napping, let the chores, phone calls, and whatever else you need to do go begging. Put your feet up and take twenty long, deep breaths. As you breathe out, imagine yourself letting go of the tension in every part of your body, starting with your head and ending with your toes. Don't forget your eyeballs, jaw, neck, and, of course, breasts. Imagine the milk flowing out of you like a gentle stream. Put on some soft music if that helps you to relax.

Finding time to relax is vital to your mental and physical well-being because the more tense you are, the harder your breasts will be. Thankfully, engorgement usually lasts no more than a couple of days.

Fissures and Cracks

If your baby isn't positioned right or doesn't latch on when you start breast-feeding, you might get cracked or sore nipples. Try changing positions and, if all else fails, call an experienced breast-feeder or lactation specialist for help (some insurance carriers now pay for lactation specialists).

Wash your breasts only with water, not soap. Don't wear plastic shields or plastic-lined nursing pads, which hold in moisture. Instead, try exposing your breasts to air as frequently as possible (without getting arrested for indecency!). I've heard that using a hair dryer on low heat (and at a slight distance) will help. Rinse your breasts after nursing to remove your baby's saliva, and then express a little milk, letting it dry on the nipples. This dried milk will form a protective coating that seems to help the healing process.

You can also apply lanolin to soothe your skin after nursing. The fissure should heal within a week. If it doesn't, consult your doctor.

Mastitis (Breast Infection)

Mastitis is an infection of the breast caused by bacteria. It results in swelling, heat, and pain, usually in just one breast or part of the breast, and may make you feel feverish or ill. If you have these symptoms, call your doctor immediately so he or she can treat you with antibiotics. Let the physician know that you are continuing to breast feed so he or she can prescribe medication that is safe for your baby. As with all antibiotics, continue to take them even if you feel better.

Don't stop nursing; this will only worsen the mastitis and cause you more pain. The baby will not be harmed by your infection since it will not change your milk's composition. If you find it too painful to nurse on the infected breast, let the milk in the infected breast flow onto a towel while you nurse on the other side. This will relieve some of the pressure before the baby finishes feeding on the infected breast.

Mastitis may be a sign that your body's immune defenses are down. Bed rest and sleep will help you recover your stamina. I know this is difficult for a new mom, so this is the time to enlist the help of your husband, partner, mother, or friend. If you don't have a good support system, you can hire a doula or baby nurse until you recover.

Incontinence

Labor and delivery can sometimes cause a temporary loss in sensation in your genitals. Don't worry if this happens to you. Leaking urine when you laugh, cough, sneeze, or jump is called stress incontinence. Needing to make frequent trips to the bathroom during the night is known as nocturnal incontinence. And the inability to hold your urine when you feel the need to go is called urge incontinence. While all of these are annoying and potentially embarrassing, incontinence will probably last for only a few weeks. If stress or frequency incontinence lasts for more than two weeks, consult your doctor. As I've said before, the best way to strengthen your pelvic muscles is by doing Kegel exercises.

Uterine Prolapse and Other Pelvic Floor Conditions

For some women, the pelvic floor muscles can become so severely weakened that they can no longer support the internal organs. When the uterus is not held in place by the pelvic floor muscles and its supporting ligaments, it can protrude into the vagina. When this happens, a condition called uterine prolapse can occur. The symptoms include the following:

Sidebar: Tummy Tucks

Some women consider having a tummy tuck (abdominoplasty) to tighten the loose skin from the middle and lower abdomen, remove excess fat, and repair the weak muscle of the abdominal wall. For those of you who are thinking about having this done, below is some information from the American Society of Plastic Surgeons (ASPS) and other experts. It's important to remember that this is major surgery, so it will leave a very large scar. Swelling, bruising, and pain are normal following the procedure, but will usually lessen within a few weeks. You might also experience numbness in the area, which can last from several months to more than a year. If you do decide to have a tummy tuck, my Tupler Technique exercises will help during the recovery period.

In a tummy tuck, the skin from the abdomen is lifted from the abdominal wall, either up to the ribs or to the navel, and excess fat is then removed. Separated abdominal muscles may be secured with sutures, depending on the size of the diastasis. Excess skin is also removed. Sometimes a new hole is created for the navel. The procedure can dramatically reduce the appearance of a protruding abdomen. But, as mentioned earlier, it does produce a permanent scar, which, depending on the extent of the original problem and the surgery required to correct it, can extend from hip to hip.

Surgical results depend on the individual patient and the surgeon. Please ask your doctor about anything you don't understand before making a decision.

Who are the best candidates for tummy tucks?

The best candidates for abdominoplasty are people who are in relatively good shape but are bothered by a large fat deposit or loose abdominal skin that won't respond to diet or exercise. The surgery is particularly helpful to women who, through multiple pregnancies, have stretched their abdominal muscles and skin beyond the point where they can return to normal. Loss of skin elasticity in older patients, which frequently occurs with slight obesity, can also be improved.

Patients who intend to lose a lot of weight should postpone the surgery until after their weight loss. Also, women who plan future pregnancies should wait, as vertical muscles in the abdomen that are tightened during the surgery can separate again during pregnancy. If you have scarring from previous abdominal surgery, your doctor may recommend against abdominoplasty or may caution you that scars could be unusually prominent.

Abdominoplasty can enhance your appearance and your self-confidence, but it won't necessarily change your looks to match your ideal, or cause other people to treat you differently. Before you decide to have surgery, think carefully about your expectations and discuss them with your surgeon.

What are the risks in having a tummy tuck?

Thousands of abdominoplasties are performed successfully each year. When done by a qualified plastic surgeon who is trained in body contouring, the results are generally quite positive. Nevertheless,

(continues)

- Feeling like your insides are falling out
- Pressure and pain in the pelvis
- An ache deep inside the vagina
- Feeling like you are sitting on a golf ball
- Constipation
- Difficulty urinating

When the muscles and tissues supporting the bladder are stretched out, the bladder will press down into the vagina, a condition known as cystocele. If the rectum bulges into the wall of the vagina from behind, you could have something called rectocele. If you experience any of the above symptoms, consult your doctor.

While all doctors will recommend doing Kegel exercises to strengthen your pelvic floor, there are several devices that can be used by your physician to monitor your condition. Femina cones are small, teardrop-shaped weights that are inserted into the vagina and held by contracting the muscles. They weigh from ten to seventy grams (the weight of a tampon being the lightest and the weight of a small drinking glass being the heaviest). You can wear them while performing your daily activities. The cones help to train yourself to pull up and in with your pelvic floor muscles.

Pessaries are doughnut-like devices that come in various shapes and sizes and are used as an alternative to surgery for a prolapsed uterus. If you have a prolapse that requires a pessary, the Kegel exercises will not be enough to rehabilitate your pelvic floor muscles, but you can still do them while wearing the device.

Pubic Bone Separation

Some women experience pain in the front of their pelvis approximately three days after giving birth. This is due to a separation or injury to the pubis, which can occur when a great deal of force is used in pushing during labor or when the baby is unusually large. This joint separation combined with a swelling in the area can cause pain while walking and, in more severe cases, an inability to walk without support. You might also notice blood in your urine from injury to the bladder or urethra.

If this happens to you, consult your doctor immediately. Treatment of this condition usually includes a modified exercise program to strengthen the abdominal muscles, so the Tupler Technique is helpful if you have this condition. Your husband or partner may not like this next part very much, but you will also be cautioned to keep your legs together as much as possible, especially when getting out of a car or out of bed. I tell my

(continued)

there are always risks associated with surgery and there are specific complications associated with this procedure.

Post-operative complications such as infection and blood clots are rare, but can occur. Infection can be treated with drainage and antibiotics, but will prolong your hospital stay. You can minimize the risk of blood clots by moving around as soon after the surgery as possible.

Poor healing, which results in conspicuous scars, may necessitate a second operation. Women's health specialist Debra Goodman, MSPT, warns, "As a physical therapist, I have seen how tummy tucks can negatively impact the musculoskeletal system. I have worked with patients who came for treatment for hip or lower back pain, which, upon examination, turned out to be due to thick layers of scar tissue. This scar tissue can be binding and can result in decreased mobility of the skin, decreased abdominal organ mobility, a tightening and weakening of the abdominal and pelvic floor muscles, and pain in the lower back, pelvis, and hip joints."

You can reduce your risk of complications by closely following your surgeon's instructions before and after the surgery, especially with regard to when and how you should resume physical activity. Smokers should be advised to quit, as smoking may increase the risk of complications and delay healing.

How should I plan for surgery?

In your initial consultation, your surgeon will evaluate your health, determine the extent of fat deposits in your abdominal region, and carefully assess your skin tone. Be sure to tell your surgeon if you smoke, and if you're taking any medications, vitamins, or other drugs.

Be frank in discussing your expectations with your surgeon. He or she should be equally frank with you, describing your alternatives and the risks and limitations of each.

If, for example, your fat deposits are limited to the area below the navel, you may require a less complex procedure called a partial abdominoplasty, also know as a mini tummy tuck, which can often be performed on an outpatient basis. You may, on the other hand, benefit more from partial or complete abdominoplasty in conjunction with liposuction to remove fat deposits from the hips, for a better body contour. Or maybe liposuction alone would create the best result.

In any case, your surgeon should work with you to recommend the procedure that is right for you and that will come closest to producing the desired body contour. During the consultation, your surgeon should also explain the anesthesia he or she will use, the type of facility where the surgery will be performed, and the costs involved. In most cases, health insurance policies do not cover the cost of abdominoplasty, but you should check your policy to be sure.

What kind of anesthesia is used?

Your doctor may select general anesthesia so you'll sleep through the operation.

(continues)

clients to move like a mermaid so they don't put stress on the pubic bone in the front or on the sacroiliac in the back.

You should also wear flat shoes. As nice as they look, high heels are not your pelvis's friend. They shorten the hamstring muscles (the muscles that run up and down the backs of your legs), which can pull your pelvis out of alignment. If you are determined to wear them, make sure you keep your hamstrings flexible. Kick those heels off as soon as you get home, or wear sneakers and flats to get to and from the office.

If your pelvic separation is serious, you might have to bind your pelvis (the same idea as splinting your abdominals) until the pubis is healed. Whatever the severity, avoid any wide separation of your legs, walking on uneven terrain, taking large strides, climbing up or down the stairs, and exaggerated pelvic movements. Heating pads or cold compresses are recommended. Do belly breaths while lying down to help relax your muscles and ease the pain.

Sacroiliac (Lower Back) Pain

The most common sacroiliac problem occurs when one side of the pelvic bone gets twisted slightly forward or backward against the sacrum. This is called a rotation.

It is simple to understand how this happens. Your body weight and the strength of the leg and back muscles that attach to the sides of your pelvis, which are used in the process of delivery, are powerful forces. Hormonal changes during pregnancy loosen the connecting ligaments. When stressed or fatigued, joints can be twisted out of place.

If you think you have this condition, consult your doctor and try to avoid the following:

- Standing up and turning while lifting something heavy
- Making love with your legs wide apart
- Sitting on a soft, squishy, and/or low chair
- Sitting in a cross-legged position
- Stepping over a child gate while carrying something heavy
- Sitting at a desk all day
- Driving a car for long distances

Since your sacroiliac joint is held together by ligaments instead of muscles, you cannot do exercises to strengthen the joint itself. But you can protect your back by taking

(continued)

Other surgeons use local anesthesia, combined with a sedative to make you drowsy. With this combination, you'll be awake but relaxed, and your abdominal region will be insensitive to pain. (However, you may feel some tugging or occasional discomfort.)

What's involved in the surgery?

Complete abdominoplasty usually takes two to five hours, depending on the extent of work required. Partial abdominoplasty may take an hour or two. Most commonly, the surgeon will make a long incision from hipbone to hipbone, just above the pubic area. A second incision is made to free the navel from surrounding tissue. With partial abdominoplasty, the incision is much shorter and the navel may not be moved, although it may be pulled into an unnatural shape as the skin is tightened and stitched.

Next, the surgeon separates the skin from the abdominal wall all the way up to your ribs and lifts a large skin flap to reveal the vertical muscles in your abdomen. These muscles may be then pulled together and stitched depending on the size of the diastasis. This provides a firmer abdominal wall and narrows the waistline. The skin flap is then stretched down and the extra skin is removed. A new hole is cut for your navel, which is then stitched in place. Finally, the incisions will be stitched, dressings will be applied, and a temporary tube may be inserted to drain excess fluid from the surgical site.

In partial abdominoplasty, the skin is separated only between the incision line and the navel. This skin flap is stretched down, the excess is removed, and the flap is stitched back into place.

How will I feel after the surgery?

For the first few days, your abdomen will probably be swollen and you're likely to feel some pain and discomfort, which can be controlled by medication. Depending on the extent of the surgery, you may be released within a few hours or you may have to remain hospitalized for two to three days. Your doctor will give you instructions for showering and changing your dressings. And though you may not be able to stand straight at first, you should start walking as soon as possible.

Surface stitches will be removed in five to seven days, and deeper sutures, with ends that protrude through the skin, will come out in two to three weeks.

What's the recovery like?

It may take you weeks or months to feel like your old self again. If you start out in top physical condition with strong abdominal muscles, recovery from abdominoplasty will be much faster. Some people return to work after two weeks, while others take three or four weeks to rest and recuperate.

Exercise will help you heal better. Even people who have never exercised before should begin an exercise program to reduce swelling, lower the chance of blood clots, and tone muscles. Vigorous exercise, however, should be avoided until you can do it comfortably. Your scars may appear to worsen during the first three to six months as they heal, but this is normal. Expect it to take nine months to a year

(continues)

One leg roll starting position.

Ending position.

Two leg roll starting position.

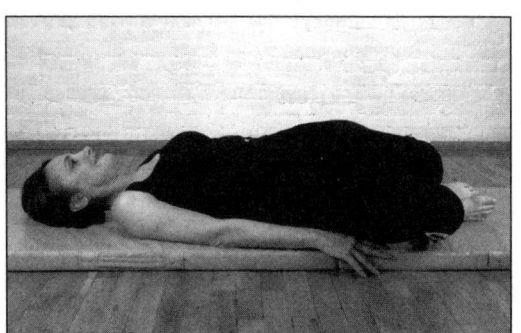

Ending position.

certain precautions, like the ones listed above, and by doing the following exercises to strengthen and stabilize the muscles that surround the sacroiliac joint:

The Leg Roll

Lie comfortably on your back with your arms out to your sides. Bend your knees, while keeping the bottoms of your feet on the floor. Holding your transverse at the fifth floor and, keeping your pelvis still, roll just one leg to the side and then back up to the starting position. Then roll the other leg to the side and back up to the starting position. Do this 5 times on each leg.

Now gently let both your legs fall to one side and then the other. Keep your feet on the floor and go only as far as you feel comfortable. The further you go, the more you stretch your lower back. This should be an extremely pleasurable exercise, so stop if you feel any pain. If done correctly, it should stretch and balance the muscles that connect

(continued)

before your scars flatten out and lighten in color. While they'll never disappear completely, abdominal scars will not show under most clothing, even under bathing suits.

What will I look like afterwards?

Abdominoplasty, whether partial or complete, produces excellent results for patients with weakened abdominal muscles or excess skin. And in most cases, the results are long lasting, if you follow a balanced diet and exercise regularly. Be realistic in your expectations and prepared for a permanent scar and a lengthy recovery period.

Keep in mind, also, that there is no guarantee that your diastasis won't open up again after a tummy tuck if you exercise incorrectly or do a jackknife getting out of bed. So even if you've had a tummy tuck, you should do the Tupler Technique in order to strengthen the abdominal muscles.

For more information about tummy tucks, visit www.asps.com or ask your physician.

the lower back to the hip bones. When these muscles relax and you balance the left and right sides, an abnormal rotation will sometimes correct itself. Change the position of your feet to stretch different parts of your back. The farther your feet are from your buttocks, the more upper-back stretch you will get. You can look in the opposite direction of your knees to get even more of a spinal twist.

Starter's tip: Remember to keep your transverse in at the fifth floor as you move. Pelvic tilts are also a great way to stretch out your lower back. See page 20 for how to do back-lying pelvic tilts.

Leg Pulls

Stand nude in front of a full-length mirror. This isn't meant to torture you, but to help you see if your iliac bones (the two bones that stick out right below your bellybutton) are uneven. If it isn't automatically obvious, put a yardstick or something similar from one hip bone to

another. If they are uneven, lie on your back holding your transverse at the fifth floor, and bring your legs up one at a time.

If your right hip bone is lower, push on the left leg while you pull on the right. If your left side is lower, push on the right leg and pull on the left. Pushing on one leg pulls the iliac bone on that side down, while pulling on the opposite leg pulls the other one up. This exercise will help counteract the strains that pulled you out of alignment in the first place.

Pelvic Push

This exercise is good for balancing the muscles on both sides of the pubic bone, and will help prevent problems in the future. Lie face-down on a comfortable surface or mat. Bring your hands up to your head, keeping your elbows bent. Bend the knee of one leg, bringing your flexed foot up as if you are standing on the ceiling. Hold your transverse in as you raise the straight leg slightly while pushing the thigh of the bent leg down into the floor. Hold for a count of 10 and repeat on the other side. Do both sides two or three times.

Pelvic Push: Good for balancing the muscles on both sides of the pubic bone.

Massage

Massage, whether it's by a professional, partner, or friend, can help soothe sore lower back muscles. You can also massage yourself by gently rolling a tennis ball or similarly sized rubber ball over the sore spots while lying on your side or stomach.

Starter's tip: Use gentle pressure and put a pillow under your hips to support your pelvis.

4

Using the Tupler Technique to Care for Other Achy Parts

UNFORTUNATELY, JOINT PROBLEMS don't always go away after you have given birth. Because relaxin, a hormone that causes your ligaments to soften and stretch during pregnancy, stays in your body for approximately six months after having a baby, your joints might still be as vulnerable as they were when you were pregnant. Whether you suffer from joint pain or not, I will show you how to strengthen your wrists, ankles, knees, and feet during this period. Some of these exercises and tips were developed by Hollis Herman, MS, PT, OCS, and Alex Pirie, authors of a terrific book called *How to Raise Children without Breaking Your Back*.

Your Last Nerve

When it comes to protecting your joints, the credo you must follow is position, position, position. This is especially true for the wrists, knees, ankles, and feet. Sitting, standing, squatting, or rising incorrectly can put serious strain on your joints during pregnancy, postpartum, and as you get older. So the first thing you need to think about from now on is posture.

Why am I talking about posture in a chapter about hands, wrists, and other joints? Your collarbones and shoulder blades together form a yoke of bones that sits around the top of your rib cage. This yoke is the platform for the muscles that move and support your head, neck, and arms. This is why a problem in your middle back can cause tingling, numbness, and weakness in your hands, head, neck, and arms.

A pinched nerve, or thoracic outlet syndrome, is one of the conditions that can be triggered by body changes during pregnancy and the early postpartum period. This condition often occurs when the ribs move up by as much as one to two inches to accommodate the growing baby. This pushes the top ribs closer to the collarbones. Even after giving birth, your muscles are still swollen with extra fluid. The smaller rib space and the swelling combine to constrict both the nerves and arteries of your arms and hands. When these nerves and arteries are pinched or restricted, you might experience symptoms in other parts of your body such as your arms and hands. Do you feel a pins-and-needles sensation or enough pain to wake you up at night? Gravity and the daily chores of parenthood can create this problem.

The good news is that stretching and exercising the muscles that attach to the shoulders, shoulder blades, and collarbones will help relieve this pain and keep you injury-free and energetic. Also try taking a warm shower and gently massaging your pectoral muscles, which run from the upper chest to the shoulder. When your shoulders are tense or pulled forward from lifting the baby, the pectorals become shortened and tight. Place four fingers in your opposite armpit, with your thumb up and fitted into the small cup-like depression where your collarbone, shoulder, and chest meet. Gently massage the muscles there.

One of most common areas of tension is in the trapezius, which is the muscle we use to lift our shoulders up. When you cradle a phone in your neck, you use this muscle. When you are tense, your shoulders probably move up toward your ears. You can relieve some of the tension that builds up in these muscles by gently rubbing them in small circles along the surface and by squeezing this muscle between your thumb and forefinger.

I highly recommend treating yourself to a professional massage. There is nothing more relaxing than a deep-tissue, full-body massage, especially for a tired mom.

Chest-Opener Exercise

Here's an easy exercise that will open up your chest, which gets pulled forward by carrying and feeding the baby. Lie on your back, on the floor or in bed, with your palms down. Holding your transverse at the fifth floor, bring your arms over your head to the floor with your palms now facing up. If they don't go very far back, put a pillow above your head and rest your arms on the pillow. Close your eyes and rest there for a bit. Take some

If your arms don't go back very far, put a pillow above your head and rest your arms on the pillow.

belly breaths and feel those chest muscles release, relax, and lengthen.

In this back-lying position, clasp your hands behind your head at the base of your skull. Now bring your elbows back as far as you can without straining. Close your eyes and breathe through the stretch as you feel the chest muscles release, relax, and lengthen. Hold this stretch for as long as you can and then relax and let your shoulders come forward again. Pressing the back of your neck on the floor will help give you more of a stretch. Repeat 4 or 5 times.

Remember to keep your elbows back when doing the chest opener.

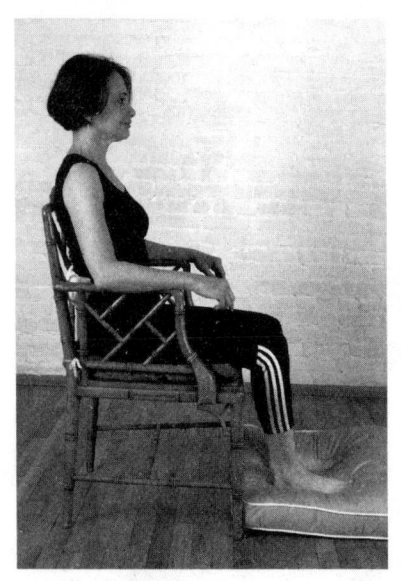

Sitting Pretty

You should always sit in a chair that does not cause stress in any part of your body. Your chair should fit you. My dream chair has a back that follows the curve of my spine, armrests slightly higher than the bottoms of my elbows to keep my shoulders from rounding, and a height such that my knees are lined up with my hips. The seat should be the length of the thigh and buttocks. If you don't have the perfect chair, then you need to make some modifications to whatever chair you do have to support your body correctly.

When sitting, your back and buttocks should be against the back of the chair. If you have lower back pain, or if you are in a chair that is too straight, you might want to put a pillow behind the small of your back. You certainly need one for your lap when feeding the baby. If you find yourself slouching, you may want to use a pillow behind your upper back. You can put your knees in the right position (lined up with your hips) by putting a cushion, stool, or phone book under your feet if they don't touch the floor, or a cushion on your seat if your knees are too high. Avoid soft chairs and deep couches that do not support your body correctly and are hard to get out of. Gliders are fine, since babies love the back-and-forth movement, but make sure you are sitting in yours properly. Sitting for extended periods is hard on your body. Frequent changes in activity and position are keys to preventing problems.

Most of us tend to hunch over when we work, care for our children, or read. The problem with this position is that the muscles begin to twitch and ache, especially in the upper back. As your shoulders round forward, the muscles between your shoulder blades stretch and become weakened. As they weaken, they become more vulnerable to stress and they force other muscles to work harder. This rounds your shoulders even farther forward. Not only is this unhealthy, it's unattractive!

Watch Your Wrists

Do you feel an ache or numbness in your wrists, tingling in your hands, or weakness in your fingers? By the end of your pregnancy you may have as much as 40 percent more fluid in your body than usual, and it may stay there for up to six months after giving birth. All that liquid creates swelling in the wrists. The combination of lifting and swelling can cause nerve compression and pain. This is called carpal tunnel syndrome. People who write on computers all day sometimes suffer from this as well. The swelling and/or repetitive bending of your wrist while lifting your baby can cause severe pain in your hands, wrists, and forearms. Although wrists are strong joints that get a lot of use in any given day, they need extra care during the early postpartum months.

You are doing a lot of lifting, some of which requires a kind of scooping-and-"cradling" gesture. In the cradle position, the wrist is flexed or curled toward your body. When you use this position over and over again, you will get a pain from what we call cradle strain whenever the wrist is bent. Another position that strains the wrist is the cocked or hammer grip, which moms use to support a sitting child or when picking up a baby under her arms. This grip pulls some of the thumb's tendon taut over bone, causing painful tendonitis. Carpenters who use this grip to hold a hammer also experience this pain deep in the wrist, or a weakness and soreness in the thumb or hand.

Make sure your wrists are not rounded like a claw or bent back when you are lifting or feeding your baby, exercising with your resistance band, or typing on a computer keyboard. Try to maintain a flat or neutral wrist position at all times. When lifting your baby, alternate sides whenever possible so that both arms and both sides of your body share the burden. If you are using the cradle grip, hold something, such as your baby's blanket, with the fingers of your lifting hand. Gripping something with your fingers will protect your wrist because you won't be able to flex all the way.

If you are using a breast pump, I recommend you get an electric or battery-operated pump instead of a manual one, which requires squeezing and puts a strain on the wrists, at least until your hands are stronger. Medela makes an excellent, multi-speed portable pump that comes in a black shoulder bag.

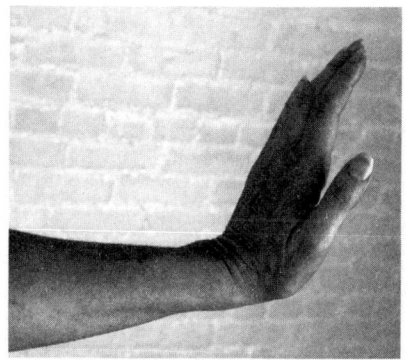

This wrist position may cause Carpal Tunnel Syndrome.

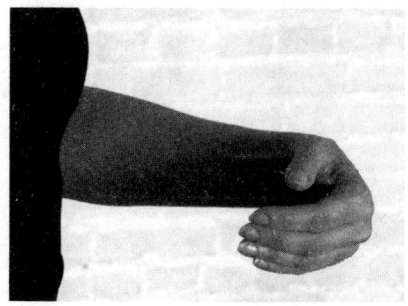

Cradle wrist.

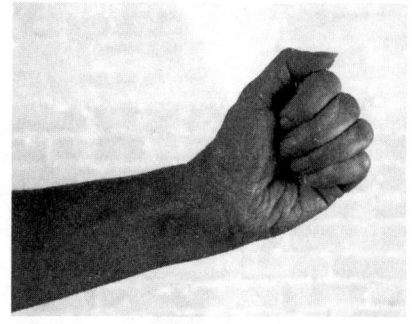

Hammer wrist.

Below are some wrist exercises that can be done just about anywhere.

Wrist Exercise #1 (Finger Lifts)

Put your whole hands and wrists on a tabletop or any flat surface with your fingers spread. Lift your pinky and put it down. Lift your ring finger and put in down. Lift your middle finger and put it down. Lift your pointer finger and put it down. Lift your thumb and put it down. Do this whenever you have your hands free and are near a flat surface. **Starter's tip:** Make sure your hands and wrists are always flat when doing this exercise.

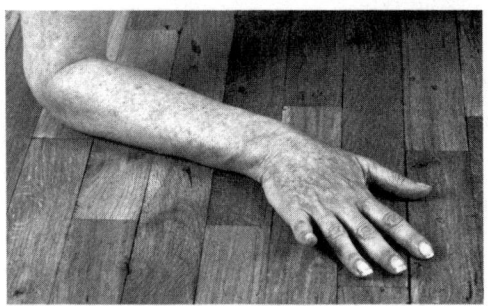 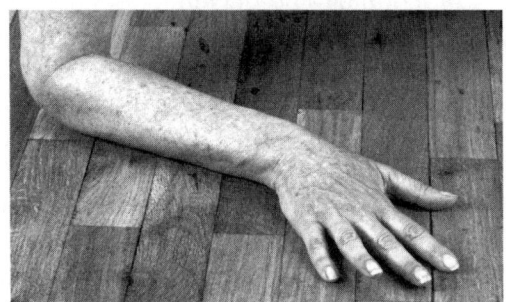

Wrist Exercise #2 (The Bag Lift)

Rest your arm on a table so that your hand and wrist extend beyond the edge, palm facing the floor. Hold a purse or shopping bag by the handle and lift it up 6 times. Do this several times a day, if possible.

　　Starter's tip: Start with a lightweight bag. As you build up strength, you can increase the weight of the bag.

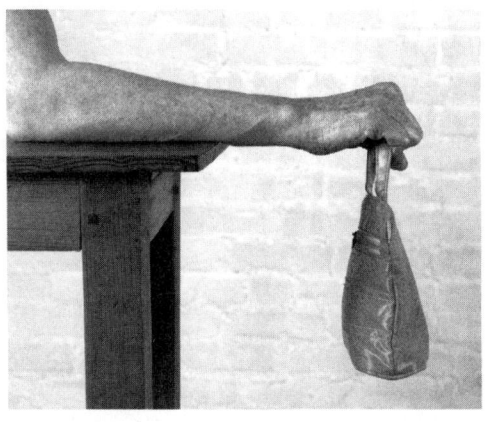 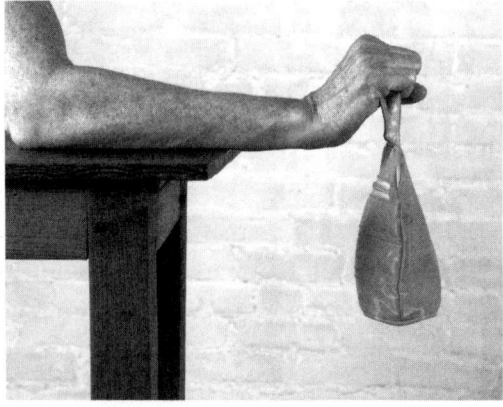

Wrist Exercise #3 (The Squeeze)

Hold a large sponge or foam ball in your hand and squeeze it. The squeeze–and–release action will pump some of the excess fluid out of your wrist and reduce the pressure on your tendons, arteries, and nerves.

Wrist Exercise #4 (Leaning Stretch)

Sit up straight in a chair, holding onto the sides with your fingertips. Tilt your head and body gently to one side until you feel a stretch in the opposite wrist. Repeat on the other side. This stretch is also great for neck strain.

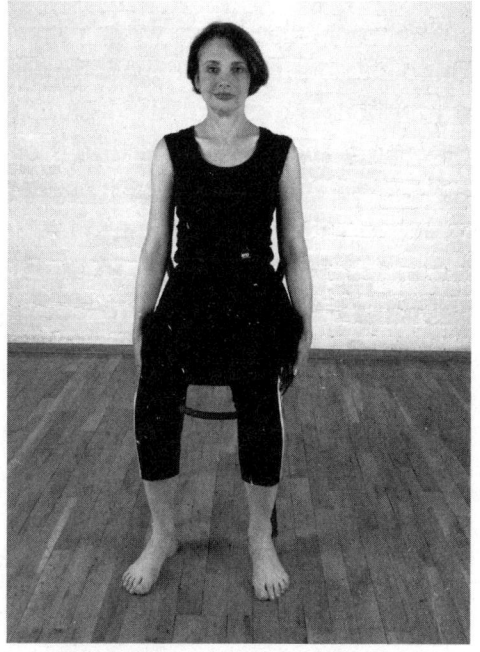

Starting position for wrist stretch.

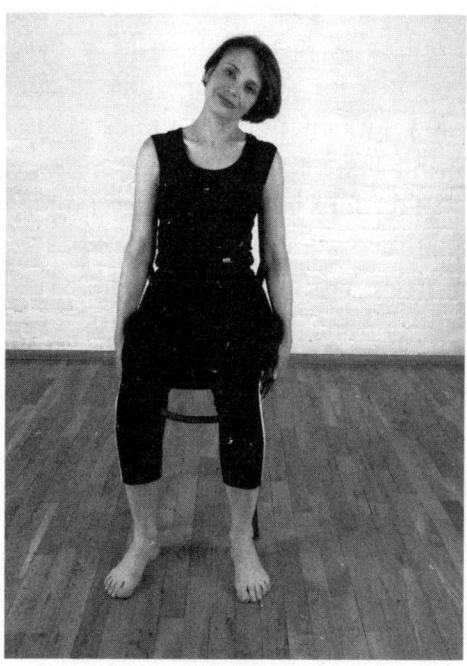

Ending position.

Needy Knees

When you were pregnant, your knees were under stress when your posture shifted to accommodate the growing baby. Hormones that loosened the ligaments also made your knees vulnerable to injury. Now that the baby is born, the extra kneeling and lifting you do adds even more stress.

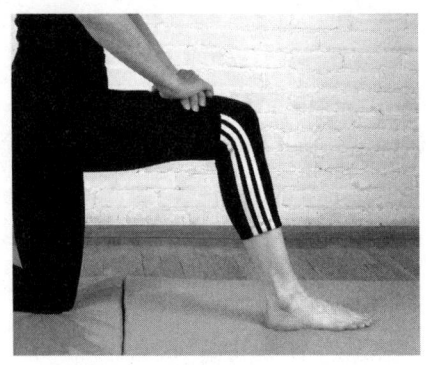

The foot should always be forward of the knee when standing up.

The knee works like a door hinge as it swings the lower leg back and forth. It doesn't allow for much twisting and turning, which is the job of the hips, ankles, and feet. When you move sideways without the use of your more flexible joints, your knee is forced to do the twisting and it ends up hurting. Did you know that most knee problems come from stiffness or stress in the muscles around the hip? Flat feet can also cause knee problems because fallen arches pull the knees inward, which puts stress on them.

You can also injure your knees when you are getting up from the floor while playing with your baby. I can't say this enough: When getting up from the floor or doing my squatting exercises, make sure your knees are in the right position, that is, never in front of your ankle bones. When you're getting up from the floor, come onto all-fours with one leg out in front of you. Bring your foot way out in front of your knee so that when your body moves forward to get up, your knee and ankle bones are lined up correctly (see photo above). Put your hands on the thigh of the forward leg (never, ever on your knee) for support as you get up.

This is why it's important to do exercises to stretch and strengthen your hips, upper legs, ankles, and feet. I have included exercises to strengthen these areas in the fifteen and thirty-minute workouts. I also want to give you a few simple knee-friendly exercises that can be done separately if you have issues in these areas.

Knee Exercise #1 (Leg kick to strengthen muscles running down the front of your thighs to your knees)

Tie the ends of your resistance band together so it forms a lasso–like circle with a diameter of about ten to twelve inches. Place the band around your ankles and sit in a chair with your back straight, feet flat on the floor. Now, step on the band with one foot and lift up the other foot with the band around your ankle, holding on to the *back* of the knee with both hands. Sit up straight, hold your transverse at the fifth floor. Go to the sixth floor as you slowly straighten your leg. Hold the leg there a moment. Then, keeping the transverse at the fifth floor, slowly bring it back to the starting position. Count out loud as you straighten your leg. Change legs. Do 10 repetitions on each leg.

Starter's tip: Make sure you do not round your back while doing this exercise. How far your leg goes out depends on your strength. Do not lock your knee when you straighten your leg. This exercise can also be done sitting on the floor with your back against the wall.

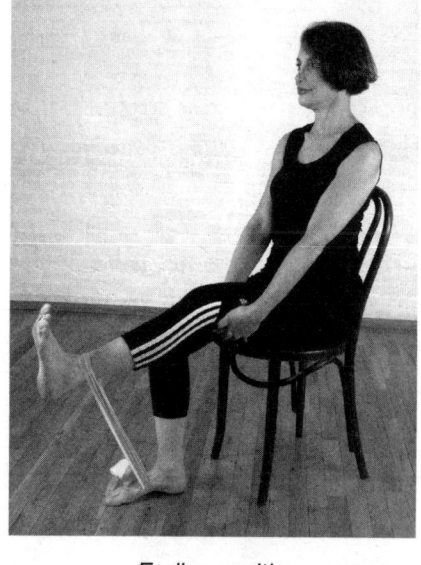

Starting position for leg kick.   *Ending position.*

Knee Exercise #2 (Leg swings to mobilize hip joints)

Stand on one leg and raise the other slightly off the floor and slightly to the front. Let your leg relax and swing your foot from side to side. If you push your fingers deeply into the center of your buttock cheeks, you will feel your hip joint moving as you swing your foot. Your knees take the stress when you have tight or weak muscles in your hips, so keeping your hip joints moving freely will save your knees. You might want to hold on to a wall for balance while doing this exercise.

Hold on to the wall for balance.

Knee Exercise #3 (Runner's stretch for the ankles and feet)

Many people like to do this stretch before a run. Lean into a wall from about three feet away. Bring one foot forward and bend the front knee, keeping the back leg straight. Now bring your transverse to the fifth floor and visualize your pubic bone moving toward your navel. Do this until you feel a stretch along the back of the straight leg.

For an additional stretch, place a sock or washcloth under the arch of the back foot. This will stretch the calf muscles as well as the foot. Relax and breathe into this stretch, then switch legs. Like the hips, the feet and ankles move more easily than the knees, so tightness here can also create stress.

Your Best Foot Forward

Your belly isn't the only thing that gets bigger when you have babies. You can expect an increase of at least half a shoe size either during pregnancy or afterwards. The extra weight and ligament-loosening hormones can cause your arches to flatten and your feet to become longer and wider.

If you find that your pre-pregnancy shoes are too short or narrow, don't fight Mother Nature. There's nothing more uncomfortable than ill-fitting shoes, plus you'll get corns, calluses, and blisters—and who needs any more unsightly appendages? Toe deformities are even more serious. Aside from being ugly, they can affect your balance and ability to walk. As beautiful as those Manolo Blahniks or Jimmy Choos look, sneakers with arch support and lots of padding under the foot are probably the best shoe choice for the new mom.

If you have extreme pain in your feet, you might want to wear foam insoles and arch supports, but make sure your shoes are large enough to support them. You can buy these in shoe, drug, and athletic-supply stores. The extra padding under your feet and arches can make you feel like you're walking on clouds! For more serious foot problems, ask a podiatrist (foot doctor) about fitting you with orthotics, which are custom-made inserts for your shoes. They can be expensive, but what price foot relief!

The exercises below will help you to put your best feet forward.

Foot Exercise #1 (Toe Curl)

Here's one you can do standing, sitting, or lying down. Point your toes so that your foot is sticking straight out, and then curl your toes under. This will stretch the top of your foot and the front of your ankles.

Foot Exercise #2 (Arches)

In a standing or sitting position, press the first knuckle of each toe into the floor and hold it there for a few seconds, then release. Next, curl your toes up like an inchworm and hold there for a few seconds, then release. Finally, put your toes and heels together and lift up your arches, making a small "O" between your feet. Hold there for a few seconds, then release. Do this 4 or 5 times. These exercises will help your falling arches and any foot pain they might be causing.

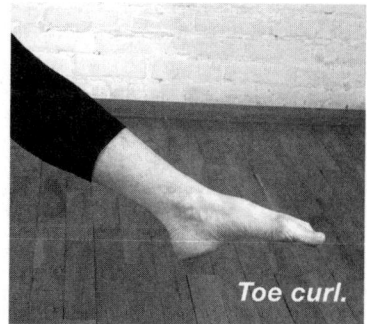

Toe curl.

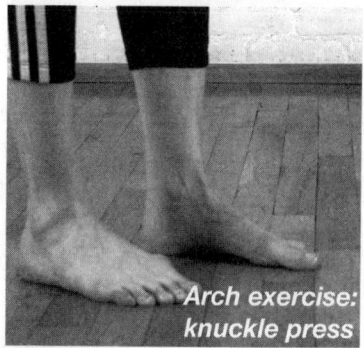

Arch exercise: knuckle press

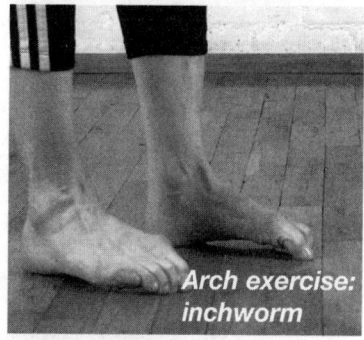

Arch exercise: inchworm

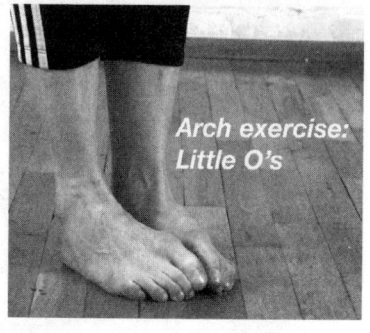

Arch exercise: Little O's

Foot Exercise #3 (Ball Rolling)

This exercise can be done with a tennis ball or a smaller rubber ball that's not too soft. Rest your bare foot on top of the ball and roll it back and forth and side to side. Let the toes curl over and grip the ball. Use whatever pressure feels right for you. You can do this either sitting (while watching TV, working at your desk, feeding the baby) or standing. Wherever you do it, it should feel great.

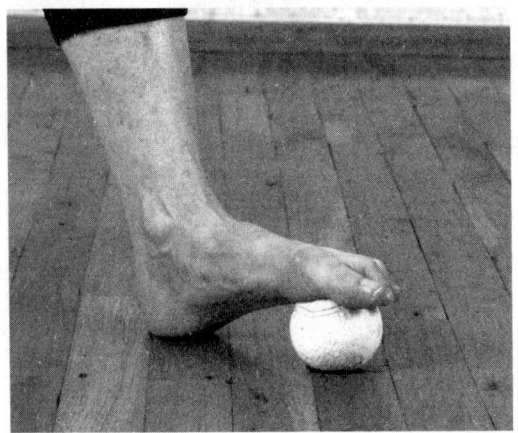
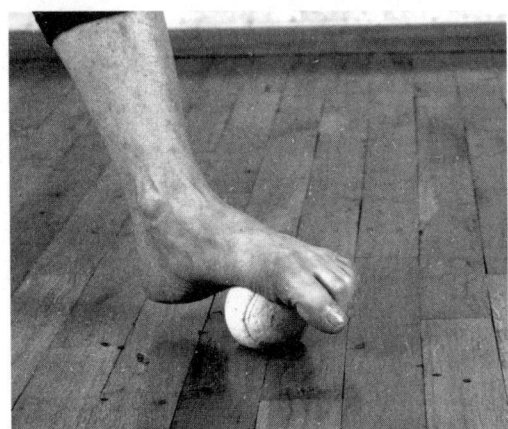

Foot Exercise #4 (Towel Grabbing)

Sit on a chair with a small towel spread out flat, toes over the nearest edge. Use your toes to grip and bunch the towel toward you until the entire towel has been folded up.

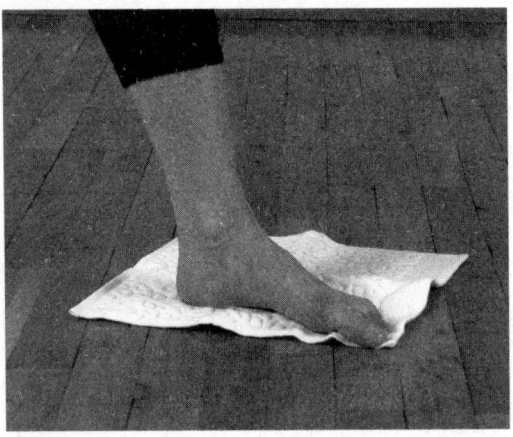
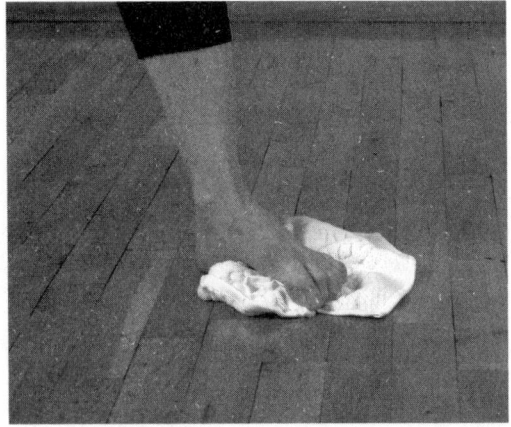

Foot Exercise #5 (Toe Grabbing)

You can raid your child's toy box for this exercise. Practice picking up marbles, small plastic blocks, or small toy cars with your toes. Use both feet and use all your toes, not just the first two.

Foot Exercise #6 (Lifting Your Feet)

Stand with your feet squarely under you. Slowly shift your weight forward, rising up onto your toes and back onto your heels and then side to side. Do this a few times.

Rankled Ankles

As I said earlier, your ankles may still be swollen with fluids after you've given birth, which is both painful and unattractive. Also, changes in your balance and weight can be rough on your ankles during pregnancy and in the early postpartum period. As a result, ankles can be easily strained or sprained during and after pregnancy. The exercises below can be done when you're lying in bed, or when sitting with your feet propped on an ottoman or glider.

Ankle Exercise #1 (Circling)

Lie on your back and prop up your calves with two pillows, letting your feet hang over the other side of the pillow. Make circles in the air with your feet. Reverse. Do this for at least three minutes. You can also do this without pillows by letting your feet stick out over the end of the bed while you rotate.

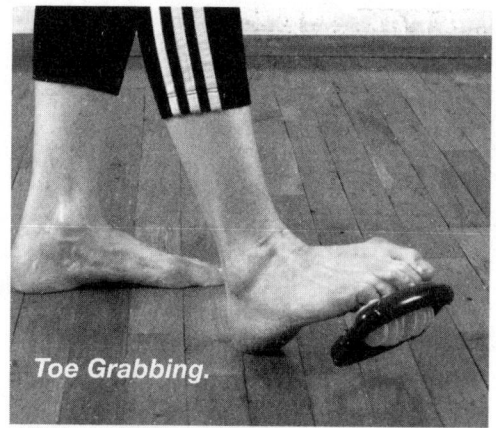

Toe Grabbing.

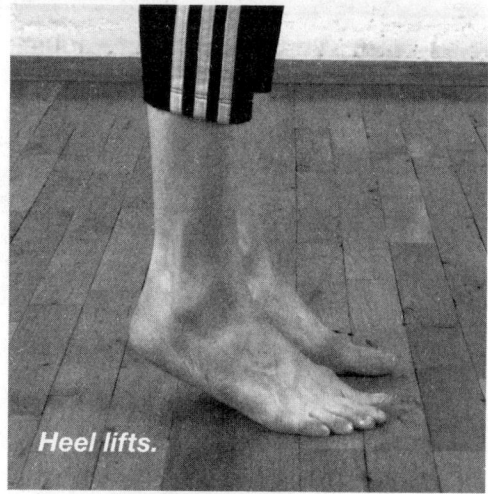

Heel lifts.

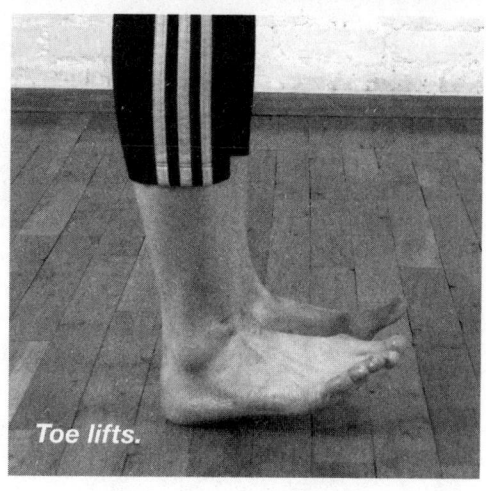

Toe lifts.

Ankle Exercise #2 (Toe Lifting)

Sit or lie with your leg supported on a pillow so that your foot is off the floor. Bring your foot up and out. Imagine stepping on the gas pedal of your car and then flex your foot in the opposite direction. As you pull back, lead with the outer edge of your foot. Build up to 50 of these a day.

Starter's tip: Once you get stronger, you can add some resistance by using your resistance band tied to an immovable object.

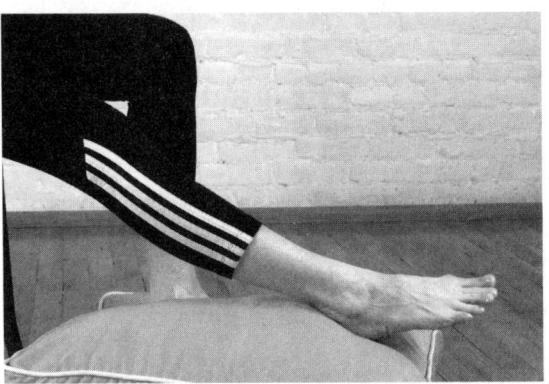 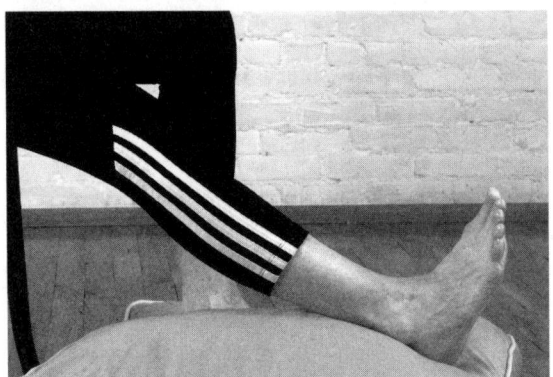

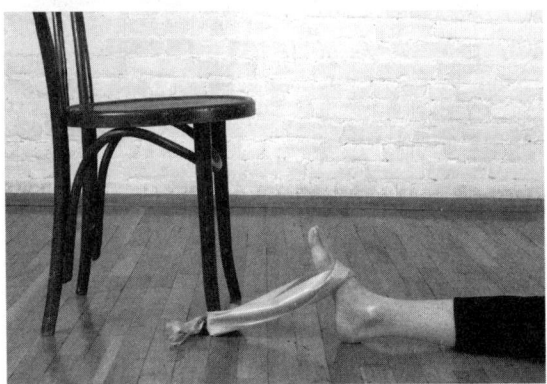 

5

The Day-to-Day Stuff: Incorporating the Tupler Technique to Protect Yourself from Injury

IN SOME CULTURES, a woman who has just given birth is surrounded by family, friends, and neighbors who tend to the daily chores for a month or more while the mother rests, feeds her baby, and gathers her strength for the task of parenthood ahead. Of course, one must pay mightily for this kind of support in my country, and perhaps yours. If you can afford it, a doula, baby nurse, or nanny will help lighten the burden of caring for you and your new baby.

Whether or not you have family support or hired help, you must develop the skills and know-how to care not just for this needy new being, but for your own well-being. Your body has been through the gauntlet and is experiencing post-traumatic stress. Taking care of your baby means lifting, twisting, bending, and standing—all of which put a tremendous strain on your back and can make your abdominal separation bigger if you do these movements incorrectly. And while you probably understood the need to be extra careful when lifting heavy objects while pregnant, it is equally important to pay attention to your back and belly once your baby has gone from a womb to a room.

I can't tell you how many new moms (including me!) have thrown out their backs while taking their baby out of the car seat, crib, or playpen. One of the things I tell my students is that it's hard to get a diastasis back together, but it's a cinch to make it bigger. One wrong move can undo weeks of transverse exercises. And the bigger your diastasis gets, the harder and longer it will take to get it all back together.

Whether you have had a C-section, an episiotomy, a tear, or twins, you probably have so many aches and pains you don't know what hurts the most! As I've said in the previous chapters, relaxin can stay in your body for up to six months after giving birth, which means you are still prone to injury in the joints. You need to be conscious at all times of how you move and what you do with your body, especially during this active postpartum period. Taking good care of yourself will enable you to take better care of your helpless little charge.

This is why we must begin this chapter by taking the Tupler Pledge: Raise your right hand and swear that your transverse muscle will become your best friend. You must promise that you will hold it in at the fifth floor for everything you do, and if you can't hold it in, you either shouldn't be doing that activity or you should be doing it differently. Okay! Now you're ready to learn the safest ways to go about your busy life, pain- and injury-free! Remember, just like in real estate where it's location, location, location, for a new mom it's correct position, position, position!

Eating and Sleeping

Well, let's hope you're doing both. During the initial two-hour feeding period you will feel a bit like a torture victim, with your defenses broken down by sleep deprivation. And you thought you were bitchy when you were pregnant! Now, you've suddenly turned into Mombie. This is why it's even more important to keep up your strength by eating right, napping when the baby naps, and asking friends and family members to look after the baby while you catch some Zs or get some leave-me-alone-time.

Your postpartum diet should consist of protein (four servings daily), fruits (three or more servings daily), vegetables (three or more servings daily), calcium (five servings daily), whole grains and legumes (five or more servings daily), fluids (at least eight glasses daily), as well as some iron-rich and high-fat foods. You might also want to ask your doctor about vitamin-mineral supplements.

If you're breast-feeding, you should increase your caloric intake to about five hundred calories per day more than your pre-pregnancy requirements. This will vary depending on your weight, since women with more fat will need fewer calories and underweight women will need more. Only a moderate amount of coffee and tea is recommended. An occasional alcoholic drink is okay. Don't flood yourself with fluids (more than twelve glasses per day) because this can slow down your milk production.

When your child is old enough to eat grown-up food, be careful about finishing his or her leftovers. I can't tell you how many moms have complained to me that they've gained weight just by clearing their toddler's plate! I know it's hard to waste good food, but it's better to wrap it up and store it than eat it yourself!

When it comes to sleep, the best way to give your body a good rest is to find the position that supports the natural curves of your spine. If you tend to sleep on your back, try putting a rolled-up towel under your neck and a big pillow under your knees. If you use a pillow, it should be soft or small enough that your chin isn't pushed up onto your chest. If you sleep on your side, place a pillow between your legs and have a good support pillow for your head so your body is completely aligned.

A full-sized body pillow or snake pillow that you can hug up close and slide between your legs will also make sleeping on your side more comfortable. Do not sleep on your stomach! It puts an enormous strain on your lower back and neck. You weren't able to sleep this way while pregnant, so don't start up again now.

Try flipping your mattress over to smooth out some of the lumps, sags, and valleys that develop with age. You might also try a Memory Foam pad on top of your mattress. The Memory Foam conforms to your body's shape, weight, and heat. Make sure that your pillow isn't so high that your neck is in an awkward position.

Getting Out of Bed

Cries of hunger at 3:00 a.m. can send a new mom bolting upright out of bed, putting a strain on her weakened or stretched abdominal muscles and lower back. Just as there is a right and wrong way to sit in a chair and get up from the floor, there is a correct way to get your tired butt out of bed. Never, ever jackknife out of bed (i.e., snap up in one movement)!

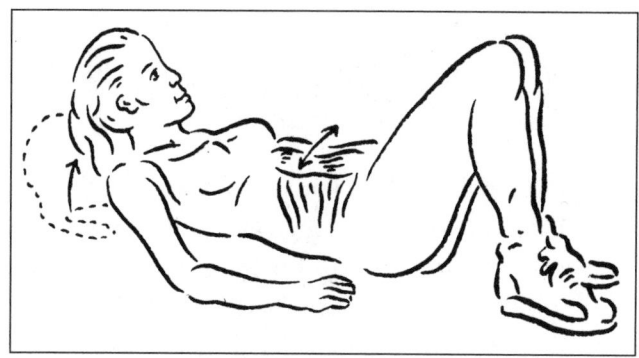

If you jackknife up from a backlying position you can make a diastasis larger.

The right way to get up from a back-lying position is to hold your transverse in without lifting your head and roll over onto your side like a log into a fetal position (see pages

If you jackknife up from a backlying position you can make a diastasis larger.

48–49). Your head should be the last thing up and the last thing down. Scoot yourself over to the edge of the bed and swing both legs over at the same time as you sit up. Put your feet on a footstool if you have a high bed or put both feet directly onto the floor. (Getting out of bed one leg at a time puts pressure on your sacroiliac and pubic bone.) After doing this a few times, you will do it without thinking.

Brushing Your Teeth

When brushing your teeth, don't lean over the sink with a rounded back. Instead, try bending from the hip with a straight back. You can also brush your teeth standing up tall, looking straight into the mirror. When it comes time to spit, put your hands on the sink for support, stick your butt out, and keep your back straight. This will give you a great hamstring stretch as well.

Getting Out of a Chair

Remember when you were nine months pregnant and you needed the jaws of life to help get you out of a chair? Well, standing up might be easier now, but it can still be a problem after sitting for long periods of time. Standing straight up from a chair puts considerable strain on the back muscles. For new moms with overstretched, post-labor or post-cesarean abdominal muscles, it is even more difficult. With this in mind, here's what you need to remember before getting up from a chair:

Slide to the front edge of the chair and place your hands on your thighs, just above the knees. Hold your transverse at the fifth floor and then rise to a hands-above-knees position. Continue to hold your transverse at the fifth floor and come up with a flat back.

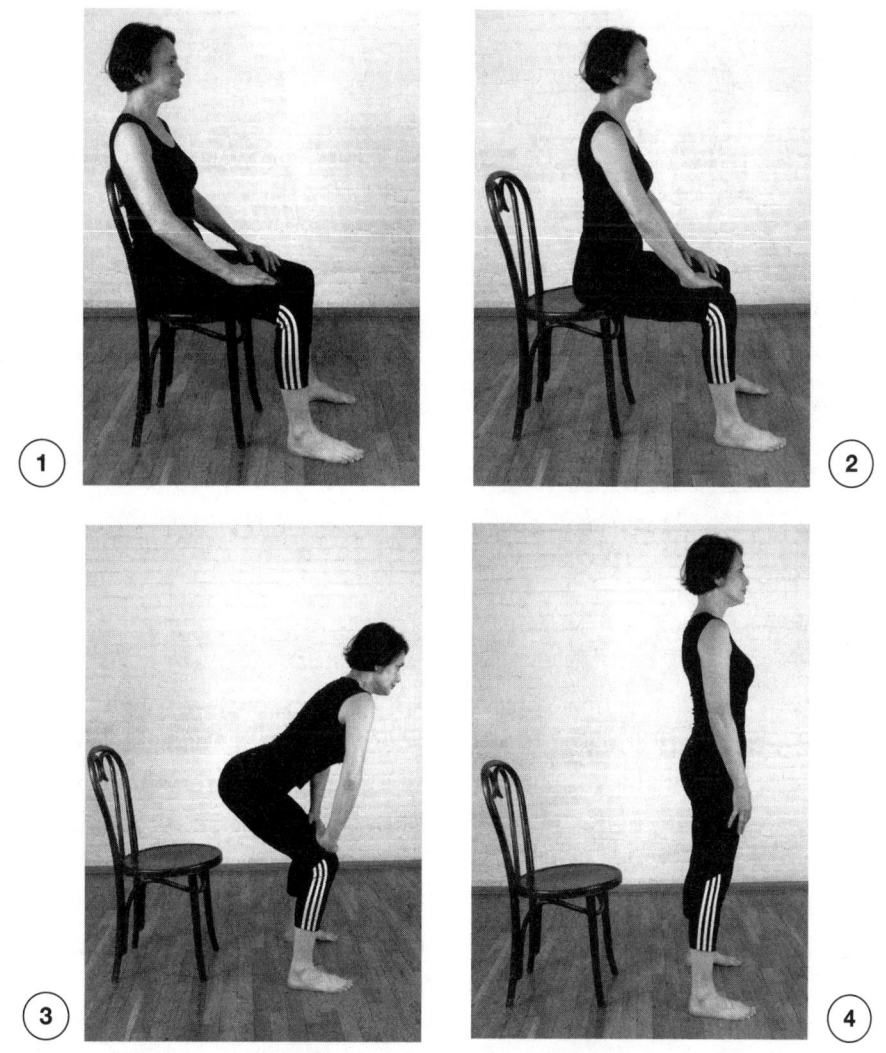

Getting up from a chair correctly.

Sneezing

Why am I telling you how to sneeze? (I showed you how to breathe, didn't I?) Because your muscles contract with a powerful reflex action when you sneeze, which puts a strain on your mid- and lower back, or pulls on your stitches if you've had a C-section. If you are under a great deal of physical or emotional stress (hello new mom!), a sneeze can also pull bones out of alignment (your bones are especially vulnerable because of your roiling hormones).

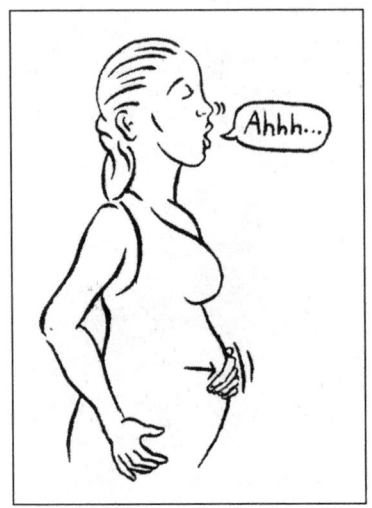

*Correct starting
position for sneezing.*

Correct ending position.

So, here's how to sneeze safely:

- The trick is to relax. When you feel the urge to sneeze, go slightly limp and let your knees relax. If you're sitting, rest your hands on your lap and relax your whole body except the muscles of your lower belly (everything from the belly button down). Take a belly breath and hold your transverse at the fifth floor before sneezing.
- Tighten both your transverse and pelvic floor muscles (to avoid leaking). You can use your hands to hold and support your ribs just below your breasts.
- When you feel a sneeze coming on, press hard at the base of your nose between your nostrils. This will give you just enough time to relax and tighten your lower abs and pelvic floor.
- When you're done sneezing, take a deep, relaxed breath. Run your fingers firmly along the bottom edge of your rib cage from the middle and out the sides. Rub your belly just above the navel. This will help relax the muscles.

Changing Your Baby

Next to feeding the baby, what's the one thing you do most frequently? It sure ain't sleeping! What goes in must come out, so knowing how to change your baby correctly (i.e., without hurting yourself) is vitally important. The first thing you must do is get the right changing table for your height. If the table is too high, it will strain your upper back; if it's too low, it will put pressure on your mid- and lower back. All changing tables, whether they are on wheels or on the top of a dresser, should be waist-high. If your changing table is not the right height for you, modify it by shortening the legs or by making it higher.

Most backaches occur when a hurrying mom snatches and lifts her child off the table. When you twist and lift or twist and lower at the same time, your muscles do battle with one another, making you vulnerable to pulled muscles, herniated discs, and even injured knees. Take it slowly and one step at a time. Here are the steps to safely get your baby from the changing table to the floor:

1. Hold your transverse in at the fifth floor as you sit your baby up, facing you. (Continue to hold your transverse in for all these steps.)
2. Bend your knees slightly, lifting your baby onto one of your shoulders.
3. Turn away from the table and put one leg behind you, bringing that knee to the floor.
4. Place your baby on the thigh of your front bent leg.
5. With a flat back, bring your baby to the floor.

Slide your toddler to the floor with a flat back.

For heavier toddlers and preschoolers, you can skip Steps 3, 4, and 5, and slide the child down your chest without bending forward, placing her on her feet. (See photo above.)

I also recommend getting a diaper bag that hangs on the side of the changing table so you don't have to bend down to get a clean diaper. When you need to dispose of a diaper, get into the hands-above-knees position. Hold your transverse in as you put the diapers in the disposal container with one hand. Come up with a flat back. It's also a good idea to have a drawer for easy access to creams, powders, and wipes. If you are really feeling pain in your back, keep a box or phone book near the table and rest one foot on it while you change the baby.

As your baby gets bigger, it will become more difficult to lift her on and off the table. Toddlers love to climb, so why not make good use of her newfound mobility by getting a step stool? Hold your toddler's hand until she reaches the top, where you can more easily lay her down flat.

If you're changing your baby on a bed—and sometimes you have to, such as when you are at someone else's house—do not stand next to the bed and bend over. Instead, put one knee on top of the bed so your back stays straight. If the bed is low enough, kneel beside it. The bed is better than the floor because you don't have to round your back so much.

Nursing Your Baby

While nursing is one of nicest ways to bond with your baby, if you don't sit correctly it can be painful in your upper and lower back. Avoid soft, squishy chairs, low couches, director's chairs, or any kind of seat that sags. When you sit with your knees above your hips, your sacroiliac joint rotates backward, putting pressure on your lower back. If your ligaments are relaxed due to hormonal changes, or if you have back problems to begin with, you are at a greater risk of causing pain.

Maintain a good sitting position using the right chair (as I discussed earlier) to support your shoulders, hips, and lower back while you nurse. Again, use a nursing pillow to bring the baby closer to your breasts (and do your Tupler Technique and/or Kegels while you breast-feed!). Never slouch forward or cross your leg in order to lift up the baby. Always alternate breasts to help keep your body on an even keel.

If you feel stiff after nursing, do this quick standing pelvic tilt. Stand approximately three feet from a wall and lean into it with your arms. Keep your legs straight and your feet hip-distance apart. Gently rock your pelvis back and forth several times. This exercise will relieve the stiffness and tightness in your lower back.

Heavy Lifting (Lifting and Carrying Your Baby)

Whether they are crawling, playing, or falling, babies spend a lot of time on the floor, and it's part of our job to pick the little buggers up. To do this safely, get down on one knee like you are about to propose marriage (you can put a pillow under your knee for comfort). Take a belly breath and hold your transverse in at the fifth floor. Put your baby onto your front bent knee and rest a moment. Then take him from your knee to your shoulder. Holding the baby with one arm, place your other hand on the thigh of your bent leg for support and stand up. Make sure your back is flat. (This technique also works for taking the baby out of an entertainment center.) Hold the transverse in at the fifth floor the whole time.

Some children like to be held close when they are carried, while others prefer to flop around. Huggers are easier to carry than squirmers because they hang on. The weight of the child pulling or leaning away from you can strain your back and stomach.

Try this technique for getting your squirmer to be more of a hugger. Bring your child's upper body close to yours with a light hug and place his hands on your shoulders. Then, grasp your child at his knees and lift. As your child leans forward, gently push his knees out slightly. This will automatically cause your child to tilt into your shoulders. Place a forearm behind his knees and keep them slightly bent by applying a gentle upward pressure. It doesn't work every time, but it could give your back the kind of break it needs.

It is also important to carry your baby in a way that produces the least strain on your wrists, back, and abs. Always remember to hold your transverse at the fifth floor when lifting or carrying your child. Here are some dos and don'ts for the most common carrying techniques:

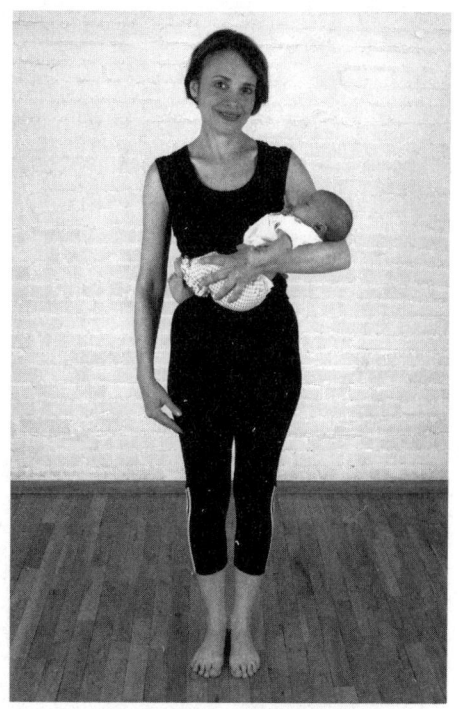

The Football Carry

This is fine for small infants, but once the little one starts putting on some pounds, carrying your baby this way can be tough on your wrists. In any case, try not to use the same side all the time, even if you have a stronger arm, which we all do. You can also hold on to a cloth or part of your baby's clothing with the fingers of your supporting hand. This will keep you from bending your wrist too far in. (See my exercises for strengthening your wrists.)

The Hip Carry

Nearly every mom uses the hip carry because it frees her up to do something with the other hand. This technique doesn't work, however, when you are doing a lot of walking. Since we tend to hike up the hip that supports the baby's weight, we can mess up our alignment. Like the football carry, make sure you alternate hips so you don't put your back out of whack.

The Front Carry

Carrying your baby in front might protect your wrists, but you won't be able to do anything else. The body-to-body contact makes it comforting for both mother and child, but it tends to make you waddle like a duck when walking, which will tire your lower back. Make sure to keep your shoulder blades down and back so you don't get that stooped-shoulder look.

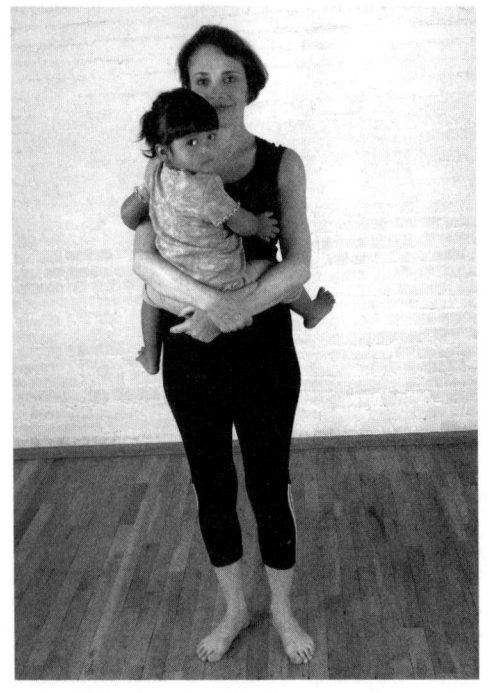

The Shoulder Carry

Carrying your baby on your shoulder is also a comforting position, but it gets increasingly harder on your back as the baby gets bigger. Balance the load by using both shoulders equally. If your baby leans away from you, see my advice above for squirmers.

The Parade Carry

If you are prone to stiff necks or have upper back problems, you should avoid lifting things above your head. Lifting your baby up high is fun (and babies love it), but it can create neck and shoulder problems. You can safely lift your baby above your head by hugging her close to your body, elbows bent. While you hug, bring your shoulder blades together and relax. Do this a few times. Then lift evenly with both arms without bending your head too far back.

Carrying an older child on your shoulders with his legs straddling your neck is great for parades and fairs, but it can bring on headaches and stiff necks, so do this for only short periods of time. After you let your child down, do a few neck stretches by bending your head slowly toward each ear and rolling it in a circle.

Carrying During Tantrums

Every parent has a horror story about when her sweet, angelic toddler spontaneously turned into a screaming, bawling, head-spinning, demon seed. It's called a tantrum. And when your child has one in public, your first reaction might be to immediately remove the child from the premises. The problem

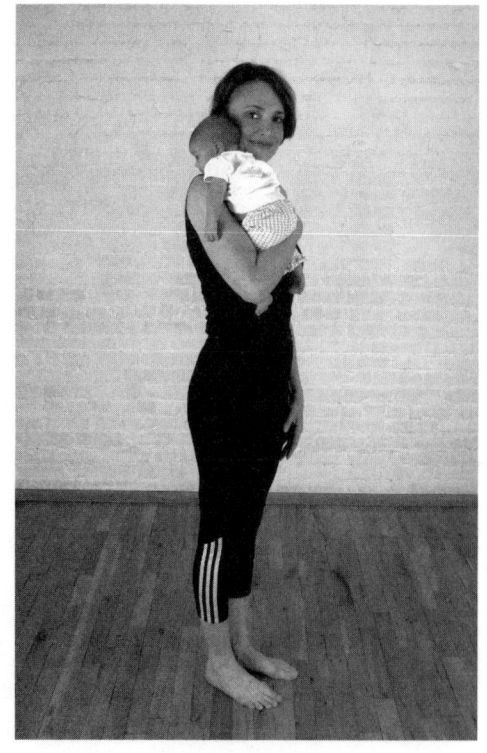

Shoulder carry.

with this is that lifting a kicking child while your body is tense is risky business for your back.

Instead of stopping and scooping, get down to your child's level (at least physically). Kneel or squat close and, if possible, hold or hug him. Don't do any lifting yet. It may seem like an eternity as you wait for him to calm down, but you will be in a better position (physically and emotionally) to pick the screamer up and take him to another location for a time-out.

The Baby and the Bathwater

Bathing the baby is not a user-friendly activity for the mom, since the only way to do it properly is on your knees. In the beginning, you can use one of those tubs that fit into the sink for infants, so you can wash your baby standing up. When they are too big for the sink, you can get a bath chair with suctions on the bottom or a baby bathtub that fits into the larger tub. Kneel close to the tub with a pillow or thick towel under your knees. If you're using a bath chair, place the chair facing sideways first and then, holding your transverse in, put your baby in the chair with her back towards you; then turn her around. Make sure everything is within reach—shampoo, bath soap, towel, toys, etc.

When it's time to dry off, turn the chair facing sideways again, place a towel on your belly, and hold your transverse at the fifth floor as you lift your baby up to your lap to wrap her up. If you have a baby bathtub, use the drainage tube at the bottom to let the water out rather than turning over the tub to empty it. Since a full tub of water is heavy, lifting it is another fine way to strain your back. If you are showering with your baby, dry yourself off before drying off your baby. You don't want your baby to slip out of your wet hands. Try these suggestions, but feel free to modify them to fit your lifestyle.

Toy Story (Picking Up After Your Child)

Nothing is more fun for babies than watching you fetch the things they throw from their play yards or highchairs. Of course, all this bending down puts even more strain on an already weakened back. Rather than rounding over to pick up toys, which most people do, get into the hand-above-knees (pelvic tilt) position. Keep one hand on the thigh of the bent leg. With your butt out, and holding your transverse in, pick up the toy with a flat back. Always come up with a flat back as well. It may seem like extra steps, but if you don't do it this way, by the time you've retrieved your three thousandth stuffed animal or sippy cup, it'll be time to call 911.

Baby Carriers

If you have an abdominal separation, you must always wear a splint (see Chapter 2) when using a front-loading baby carrier because the pressure from the baby's weight will pull your abdominal muscles further apart. Front-loading carriers, especially when worn too low, also cause some women to curve their upper backs. The same goes for backpack carriers when the baby gets older, although it's not as crucial to wear a splint with these because the baby carrier isn't pressing directly on the abs.

Be careful putting the backpack on and taking it off. Get someone to help you whenever possible. If you're putting on a baby-filled backpack by yourself, place it first on a secure high surface like a bed, car hood, or table. (You can wrap the metal at the bottom of the backpack with duct tape to keep it from scratching delicate furniture or cars.) Make sure you use the pack's waist strap so that some of the weight is distributed onto your hips and off your back.

Slings allow you to shift the weight of the baby from front to back, or side to side, but they will distort your posture if you use them for long periods of time, since you must compensate for the extra weight. If you use a sling, make sure that you alternate sides each time you use it. You can also switch from back to front.

Quick Carrier Exercise

Shrug your shoulders and roll them back before and after using a backpack or front-loading carrier. This movement stretches out the muscles across the front of your chest and counteracts the pulling forward of your shoulders while carrying the baby. Plus, it feels really good!

Car Seats

I pulled my back out getting my daughter out of her rear-facing car seat. I was rushing, so I leaned over and twisted. I heard my back snap, even though I was holding in my transverse! It just goes to show you that even experts can injure themselves. I will never make that mistake again. Now, I always put one foot in the car, bend both my knees, unsnap the straps, and lift my daughter from behind the seat, rather than facing her, to avoid torquing. Then, holding my transverse in, I lift her up with her butt facing me.

If you prefer putting the car seat in the middle of the back seat, you can sit next to your child while you lift him onto your lap. You can then slide over to the door, swing both feet onto the street, and hold your transverse in as you stand up with your child held close to your chest. The problem with this is that most mothers I know put the car seats on the sides close to the door for quick access. Experiment to see what works best for you.

Portable Car Seats

Portable car seats may be convenient, but they are unwieldy to carry and I don't recommend them. Between their shape and the weight of the baby, you must hold them to the side, far from your center of gravity. Most people carry them in the crook of their elbows, which places the wrist at a dangerous angle, especially if they are holding a diaper bag or purse in that hand as well. Instead, carry the car seat in one arm while carrying your baby in the other arm next to you. If you must carry the seat with the child in it, alternate sides frequently to give your muscles a rest.

High Chairs

Always get your baby in and out of the high chair from behind. Lifting him from the front forces you to slouch over without supporting your back. The same goes for taking him out: Go behind the chair, unsnap the straps, bend your knees, hold your transverse in, and lift your baby straight up, bringing him towards your chest before sliding him down your body on the floor. When your child gets a little older, have him stand up before you take him out.

Cribs

The best kind of crib is the high-standing kind with sides that drop. Always take down the side of the crib before getting your baby, even if you're in a hurry. Never round over to take your baby out of the crib and always pull in your transverse and keep your knees slightly bent when lifting your baby in or out of the crib.

Portable Cribs and Play Yards

Getting your baby out of a portable crib or play yard can be tricky, since they are low to the ground. Start by getting down on both knees. If your baby is lying down, gently roll or slide her to the side of the crib closest to you. Sit her up and then, if she's old enough, stand her up. Holding your transverse in, lift her to your chest near your shoulder, holding onto the play yard with your other hand for support. Holding your transverse in at the fifth floor, lift yourself up with a straight back (no slouching over). You can also buy supports that fit under the legs of the crib to make it higher. (Studies have shown that it's easier on the back to lift something that is at least twelve inches above the ground.)

Swings and Bouncy Seats

Every mother knows how a swing or bouncy seat can provide some peace and peace of mind while preparing dinner, cleaning house, or whatever necessitates your leaving the room for a minute. As wonderful as these mother's helpers are, you must use caution when taking your child in and out of them. If the swing is at knee- or shin-level, you won't be able to get close enough to safely lift your child in and out of the seat. Stooping or bending over can put a tremendous strain on your back and knees.

A safer way to do this is to kneel on one or both knees before putting your baby in or taking her out. It may seem harder or take a second longer to get down on the floor, but it's easier on your body in the long run. You can also try putting your baby into the swing by sliding her in from behind. Standing closer allows you to squat, rather than stoop, as you lower or lift. Need I remind you again to hold your transverse in while lifting the baby? I didn't think so.

Strollers

The old-fashioned baby carriage that your mother or grandmother used (the kind with the hood, sometimes called a pram) was the perfect height for lifting an infant in and out without straining your back. Today's strollers, while lightweight, collapsible, and far better for getting in and out of a bus or onto a mall escalator, or folding into a car trunk, force us to stoop over in order to get a child in and out of the seat. Hello aching back! Try to find a stroller that is high enough that you can stand up straight without slouching while holding on to it.

The best way to put your child into a stroller is to squat or kneel in front of it and slide your baby in. You can kneel on one or both legs, whichever is more comfortable. You can use a towel or piece of foam rubber, keeping it in the storage space below the stroller or in the net bag for easy access. To take your baby out of the stroller, squat or kneel in front and slide him into your arms before standing up. I know this takes a minute or two longer, but is saving a minute worth breaking your back?

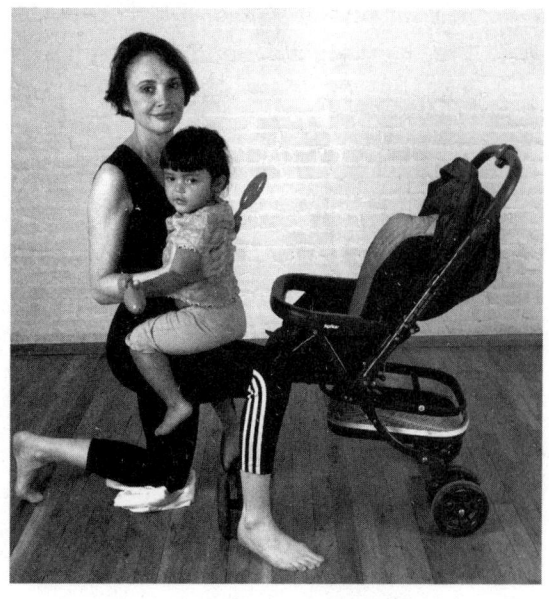

I suggest you buy the simplest, sturdiest stroller that you can find. If you can afford it, a good bet is a new ergonomically correct stroller called Stokke Xplory, which is one-third higher off the ground than the average baby buggy. It has five different positions, it's easy to maneuver up and down steps, and you can remove your baby or toddler without bending over. You can order one by going to stokkeusa.com.

Speaking of going up and down steps, resist the temptation to lift the entire stroller and child. Instead, use the back wheels of the stroller to pull the baby up short flights of stairs by walking up backwards and pulling up step-by-step. You can do the same coming down the stairs by slowly lowering the stroller onto the back wheels. Of course, always keep your transverse in while doing any of the above. Ask someone for help if you are in a hurry.

Diaper Bags/Purses

Use a diaper bag with a strap that is long enough to wear across your chest. Diaper bags with shorter shoulder straps will inevitably fall off when you bend down or reach for the baby. I happen to like backpack diaper bags that give you hands-free access.

Telephones

Speaking of hands-free, I strongly recommend getting a hands-free phone so you don't get a stiff neck or pinched nerve from cradling the phone in your shoulder. Attach the phone to your belt or get a fanny pack to carry it around your waist. Putting the phone in your pocket won't work because it will keep falling out whenever you bend down. Free hands allow you to change, feed, or cuddle your baby while you talk on the phone. Most cell phones come with microphones and ear attachments.

Child Gates

Child gates that open and close (the only kind you should get) are a great way to isolate any part of your home or apartment that might be dangerous for an infant or toddler, such as stairs and kitchens. While gates will protect a curious crawler, they can pose a threat to the postpartum mom. In the course of a busy day, we are often tempted to save time by stepping over the gate instead of opening it. Don't do it! A bad leg lift can put stress on your pelvis and push your sacroiliac joint out of place. As I discussed in Chapter 3, if you already have a pelvic or lower back problem, you must never, ever step over a gate—or anything high, for that matter.

Always open your child gate, especially if you are carrying something heavy like wash or a baby. It may take a bit longer, but it can save you hours or days of agony!

Grocery Injustice

In addition to picking up your baby, one of your most frequent weight-lifting motions is probably taking your groceries out of the trunk of your car. As when you're lifting your baby, pick the bags up with your transverse in and with a flat back. You can also try this technique:

- Get your feet as far under the car as possible.
- Bend your knees, take a belly breath, pull your transverse in.
- Lift your grocery bag on to the edge of the car.
- Reposition yourself so that you can lift the weight close to your body. Remember to keep the natural curve in your lower back.
- Pull your transverse in each time you lift.

Getting In and Out of the Car

Most of us are in a hurry, so we jump in and out of a car like we're Dale Evans Jr. on the raceway. A far safer way is to back into the car seat, knees together, head facing outside. Then pivot, bringing both knees in together. Reverse for getting out. Once you get the hang of it, this method will take no time at all!

Make sure your car seat isn't too low or tipped so far back that your knees are higher than your hips. Sit on a firm cushion or place one behind your back so that your thighs are parallel to the floor.

6

Getting Your Life Back: Protecting Your Newly Reduced Mummy Tummy When Doing Other Exercises

NOW THAT YOU'VE RECOVERED from the birthing experience, and have done some or all of the exercises in this book, you probably feel ready to return to the life you enjoyed before your pregnancy. You and your partner might even be thinking about sex again, (although, truth be told, most new moms would rather have six hours of uninterrupted sleep than six orgasms). The problem is, while you might be psychologically ready, there are still some physical precautions you must take.

First, most obstetricians recommend waiting six weeks before exercising vigorously or having intercourse. It's important that your cervix has healed and that bleeding has stopped. As I discussed earlier, you might also find intercourse painful if you've damaged your perineal area. Women who have had cesareans, episiotomies, or severe tears often must wait months until their stitches are healed. Plus, sex takes energy, which is in short supply right about now. Rest assured: You *will* have a sex life again one day, even if your libido is currently on hiatus. Whatever your condition is, you need to check with your physician before you either restart or start a new activity.

Some women find that breast-feeding fulfills their needs for physical intimacy during this period, while others find comfort in snuggling, kissing, caressing, and oral sex with their partners. Parenting can put a strain on a relationship, but it can also be a shared blessing. (Is there anything sexier than a loving, nurturing daddy?) If you are physically and emotionally ready to have sex again, you might have to make appointments for sex around the baby's nap schedule. Sex is fun whether it's planned, spontaneous, on Saturday afternoon, or on Saturday night!

As for getting back to your old exercise routines, remember my mantra: Your abdominal muscles are the foundation of everything that you do, so you need to incorporate the Tupler Technique in whatever sport or workout you choose. If you can't hold your transverse in while doing a particular exercise, it is an indication that you shouldn't be doing it! And, as you know, the relaxin hormone you had while pregnant stays in your body for up to six months after giving birth, which means that you are still at risk of injury if you don't exercise correctly.

The good news is that there are exercise programs for postpartum moms, such as Stroller Strides and Stroller Size, as well as yoga classes that you can do with your baby in tow. These classes are terrific because they get you out of the house and help you bond with your baby as well as with other new moms. Don't take classes that require you to wear a front-loading carrier, or wear a splint if you must. The bad news for tennis players, golfers, and skiers is that these sports, which involve a lot of forward crossover twisting, can undo all the good mummy tummy work you've done thus far. They are also hard on the wrists and ankles. The same goes for racquetball and paddleball. As much as you might love these sports, once you've closed your diastasis, you can pull out your rackets, paddles, skis, and clubs.

Here are some guidelines for safe postpartum exercising. In the next chapter, I'll describe a Thirty-Minute Tupler Workout that you can do at home.

Aerobics

Although you will want to wait six weeks after giving birth before resuming any high-impact aerobic classes or running, this doesn't mean you can't take brisk walks. In fact, walking is one of the best exercises you can do. Since every person's fitness level is different, the time to resume these workouts depends on what you were doing before and during your pregnancy. In the beginning, exercise briefly and frequently rather than doing one long session. This helps tone the muscles better. Also, protect your ankles by wearing shoes that support your arches and ankles.

Stabilization Balls

The golden rule of tum is that you should wait until your diastasis is repaired before doing back-lying abdominal exercises on a stabilization ball, those large, colorful rubber balls you find at most gyms. Once you start using the balls again, be careful not to jack-knife off the ball. Instead, hold your transverse in and roll yourself down to a sitting position on the floor without lifting your head.

Sit-ups and Crunches

Beware of crossover abdominal exercises, such as those for your obliques (the middle layer of abdominals, which I discussed earlier), where the right side of your body lifts to the left and vice versa. This forward-crossover movement will most certainly make your diastasis bigger. Likewise, don't do full sit-ups, crunches with your shoulders off the ground, knee-chest exercises, or double-leg lifts, as they will make your diastasis larger or *create* a diatasis if you don't already have one!

Swimming

Swimming is a great way to exercise all the muscles in your body without stressing the joints, but it's best to wait the six weeks before swimming because you may still be bleeding and open to infection. Avoid the frog kick (where your knees open wide and then close), which puts pressure on the pubic bone. Do the flutter kick instead. Also, be careful getting in and out of the pool; always get in and out with your legs together. And remember to keep your transverse in at the fifth floor as you take each stroke.

Yoga

Avoid backbends such as the bridge pose, which will make your abdominal separation bigger. You should also be careful with positions such as the downward dog and handstands, which put a great deal of pressure on your wrists. If your wrists hurt, stop immediately. You might also want to avoid forward twists, although twists that pull your shoulder away from your body are okay. Otherwise, yoga is a great way to relieve stress and build strength during and after pregnancy.

Pilates

Pilates, which is designed to work the core abdominal muscles, can be risky if you are doing back-lying exercises where your shoulders are higher than your hips because you are not able to engage your transverse muscle. Examples of Pilates mat exercises to avoid are the 100s, roll-ups, rollovers, rolling like a ball and a seal, the single-leg stretch, the double-leg stretch, the corkscrew, the jackknife, the teaser, and the neck pull. Crossover exercises like the saw are equally risky. The seated upper body and side-lying exercises done on Pilates machines (the ones with the springs) are great and safe to do.

Strength Training

New moms still have muscle imbalances left over from pregnancy, so keep the following in mind while you are lifting weights. During pregnancy, as your breasts get bigger, your shoulders come forward and your chest muscles get short and tight while your upper back muscles get long and weak. This results in the rounding forward of your shoulders. This is why you don't want to do weight-bearing exercises that involve rounding your chest. You want to do more upper back than chest work.

When working your chest, avoid exercises that bring hand weights together in front of your chest. A better way to build up chest strength is by doing push-ups either on the floor or against the wall. Your goal is to shorten the upper back muscles that have been stretched out. Remember to hold your shoulder blades down while working the back and chest. This will help get rid of those unattractive rounded shoulders.

Also, always use slow, controlled movements to lift instead of using momentum. Never swing or jerk your arms in order to lift heavy weights. (The key to doing this is to hold your transverse in while lifting, which will slow you down.) Remember to exhale during the exertion, bringing your transverse back toward your spine. Rest briefly between exercises. This is a great time to do a Kegel exercise! Remember to protect your wrists while lifting weights by keeping them in a flat position (thumb stays on top), and to protect your knees by keeping them lined up with your ankle bones when doing squats.

Biking and Spinning

It's a no-brainer that sitting on a bike too soon after childbirth can be painful. Even if you are all healed, you might want to get a gel seat or special biking pants to make biking more comfortable. Make sure the seat is at the correct height to protect your knees. Be careful if you have wrist pain, because using low-riding handlebars on racing bicycles puts a lot of pressure on the wrists. If you're spinning and you have wrist pain, raise the handlebars up higher and put most of your weight on your legs rather than your arms. Be careful not to round your back while leaning forward. Keep your back straight and elbows bent.

Step

Use a low step at first, and avoid the wide open leg movements that put stress on the pubic bone.

Stretching

As with weight training, always use slow, controlled movements—never bounce in a stretch. Always relax the muscle you are stretching and breathe through the stretch as you visualize that muscle lengthening. Focus on lengthening the muscles that have been shortened, such as the lower back muscles, hip flexors, chest muscles, and hamstrings. Avoid open leg stretches if you have any pubic pain. Hold each stretch for at least thirty seconds.

7

The Thirty-Minute Tupler Workout

THE FIRST ELEVEN EXERCISES below are a warm-up, and are similar to the ones you did for the fifteen-minute Tupler Workout. Remember, if you don't make it all the way through these exercises, always end with breathing/relaxation. Also, remember to do some Kegel exercises in between sets while you are resting!

1. Neck Stretch (one minute)

Sit in a chair or on the floor. Straighten your neck and drop your chin gently. Hold this position as you take your right hand and place it on the left side of your head above the temple. Gently bring your right ear toward your right shoulder, using your hand as a weight to stretch the left side of your neck. Close your eyes and slowly move your left shoulder toward the floor. Do this for thirty seconds on each side by counting very slowly to thirty.

Starter's tip: Make sure you do not jut out your chin as you are doing these exercises. Keep your shoulders relaxed.

2. Shoulder Circles (fifteen seconds)

You can do this exercise while sitting in the chair. Roll your shoulders back in full circles 8 times. Try not to roll forward because new moms tend to round their shoulders forward when holding, feeding, or changing the baby.

3. Crossover Arm Stretches (one minute)

Take one arm straight across your chest, holding onto the wrist with the other hand. Now relax both shoulders. Turn your head toward the shoulder you are stretching. Close your eyes and move the shoulder that you are now facing down toward the floor. Hold for thirty seconds and repeat on the other side. You should feel this stretch behind your shoulder.

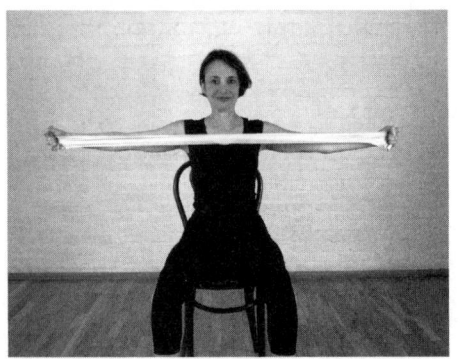

4. Chest Stretch/Upper Back Strengthening (one minute)

Sitting straight up in your chair, hold your resistance band in both hands, grabbing about an inch in your fists on each side. (The shorter you make the band, the more difficult the exercise.) Place the band on your chest above your breasts, keeping your wrists flat. Take a belly breath, and pull your transverse in to the fifth floor. Continue to hold it at the fifth floor as you straighten your arms out to the side. Your shoulders should be lined up with your wrists. Keep your elbows straight but soft and your shoulders down and relaxed. Think about energy flowing down your arms and out of your knuckles. While holding this position, do 30 contractions with your abs from the fifth to the sixth floor. Count out loud to 30. Rest for a moment and then do another set.

Starter's tip: Make sure you don't arch your back. In this exercise, your chest is getting longer and your upper back muscles are getting shorter. Also, keep your shoulders relaxed.

5. Seated Transverse (five minutes)

Sit up straight in your chair, placing one hand under your breasts and the other one on your bellybutton. Take a belly breath and expand your belly to the first floor. Now bring your bellybutton from the first floor to the fourth floor. This is your starting position. (I am assuming you have been doing the transverse exercises and are now ready to progress to the fourth floor.) Now bring your bellybutton to the fifth floor. As it moves back toward your spine, imagine your ribs coming together. Squeeze and hold it a moment at the fifth floor as you count out loud. Then release it to the fourth floor before starting the next repetition. Do 100 squeeze-and-holds. If you're counting out loud, I know you're breathing! You should feel this exercise in your back and your abdominals. End each set with a belly breath, bringing your bellybutton all the way back toward your spine once more as you exhale. One set is 100 contractions. It takes two-and-a-half minutes. If you get out of breath while doing this exercise, slow down and count out loud with more volume in your voice.

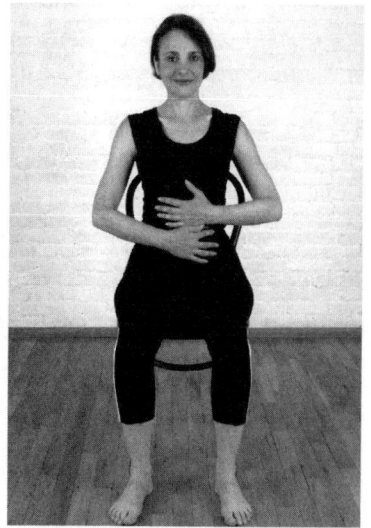

Position of hands without splint for the seated transverse exercise.

For the second set of 100, let's make this exercise a little bit harder. Contract from the fifth to the sixth floor. These contractions are isometric or very small squeezes where you see no movement of the abdominal muscles. Do this second set with a splint. Follow these five steps when wearing a splint:

a. Place the splint on your back at waist level, with the terry cloth side close to your body.

b. Cross your arms in front of your body. With your right hand, using an overhand hold, pull the splint on the left side of your body (at waist level) toward your bellybutton.

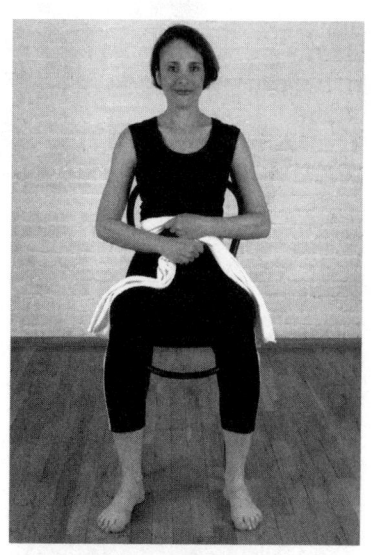

Position of hands with splint.

c. With your left hand, using an overhand hold, pull the splint on the right side of your body (at waist level) toward your bellybutton. This hand will be underneath the right hand.

d. Your hands should be resting on top of your recti muscle. You can then feel the backward movement of the muscles when engaging your transverse muscle.

e. Relax your shoulders as you are holding the splint.

Now that you have your splint in place, you are ready to do the second set. Expand your belly and bring your transverse to the fifth floor. Hold your transverse at the fifth floor as you pull the two halves of the splint together, so your hands are now resting on your abdominals. You will hold the splint together for all 100 contractions from the fifth to the sixth floor. (Do not pull with each contraction.) Bring your elbows to your side and relax your shoulders. Now do the 100 contractions from the fifth to the sixth floor, counting out loud. Remember, you should see no movement, as these are isometric squeezes. You should feel this exercise in your back and your abdominals. End with a belly breath. Don't forget to bring the transverse to the fifth floor on as you exhale.

6. Abdominal/Transverse Exercise on All-Fours (fifteen seconds)

Get down on all-fours, palms flat on the floor, knees hip-distance apart, toes touching the floor. Keeping your back flat and still, bring your transverse to the third floor. This is your starting position. Now bring your bellybutton toward your spine at the fifth floor. Squeeze and hold it there a moment, then release to the third floor before you start the next repetition. Count out loud as you do 15 contractions from the third to the fifth floor.

7. Table-Top/Hamstring Stretch (thirty seconds)

From a standing position, hold your transverse at the fifth floor as you slide your hands from your upper thighs to your lower thighs just above your knees. Keep your knees straight without locking them, and your back flat. Do not stick out your chin. This exercise stretches your hamstrings (the muscles in the back of your upper legs). Count out loud with your hands resting on your thighs just above your knees as you do 15 transverse contractions. Holding your transverse at the fifth floor, come up to a standing position with a flat back. Repeat.

8. Standing Hip Flexor Stretch (one minute)

This exercise is sometimes called the runner's stretch. Stand with one leg in front of the other, hip-distance apart, with the back leg straight and the front leg bent. The distance between your legs should be about eighteen inches. Make sure your knee is not forward of your anklebone. For balance, you may want to hold on to a wall or secured chair while doing this stretch. Keeping your back leg straight and your transverse in at the fifth floor, think of bringing your pubic bone toward your navel. Hold it there for a count of fifteen. Now do the other leg. You should feel this stretch at the top of your leg. My hand in the photo is on the hip flexor, which is where you should feel this stretch.

9. Standing Quadricep (Front of Thigh) Stretch (one minute)

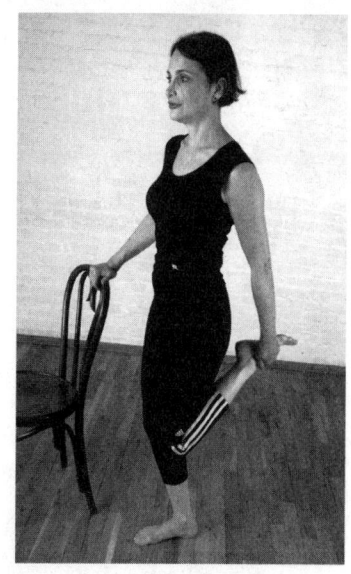

Do this stretch whenever you do the runner's stretch. Since you will be standing on one leg while you are stretching the other leg, you may want to hold on to a wall or secured chair with the hand on the same side as the supporting leg. The supporting leg should be slightly bent. Hold your transverse at the fifth floor as you bring your other leg into the air, thinking about bringing your heel toward your buttocks. Hold the front of your foot or your ankle with your other hand. Make sure your knees and legs are together, with the bent knee pointing down to the floor. Now hold the transverse at the fifth floor and think about bringing your pubic bone to your bellybutton. Hold it there as you count out loud to fifteen. Hold your transverse at the fifth floor as you put your leg back on the floor. Change legs.

If you do not have the flexibility to hold on to your ankle, you can put a belt or scarf around your foot and hold on to the ends to pull up the bent leg. You can also put your foot on a chair behind you. If you do not feel the stretch, you need a chair with a higher seat. In both cases, make sure the supporting leg is bent and the knees are together. Hold your transverse at the fifth floor, think of bringing the pubic bone toward your bellybutton, and count out loud to fifteen.

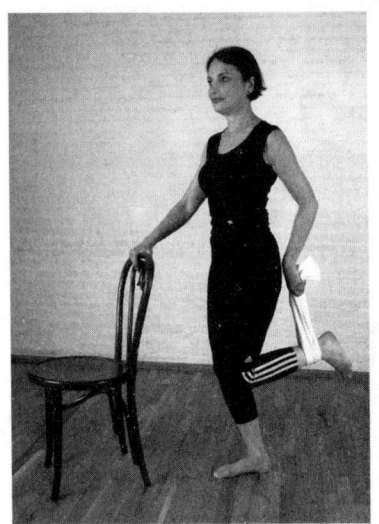

Quadricep stretch with scarf.

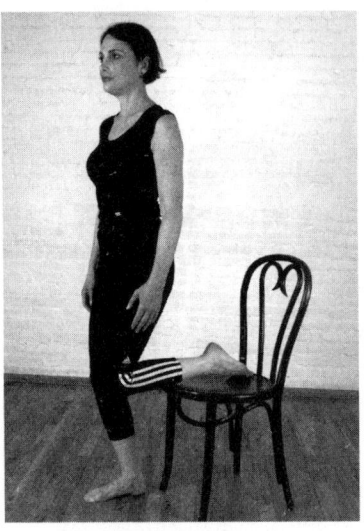

Quadricep stretch with chair.

10. Back of Leg Stretch (one minute)

Sit on the edge of your chair with one leg bent and one leg straight. Flex the foot of the straight leg (toes toward the ceiling), keeping the back of your leg straight. With your transverse at the fifth floor, lean forward with a flat back, keeping your hands on the thigh of your bent leg. Go as far as you can until you feel the stretch. Stick out your butt to get even more of a stretch. Do not jut out your chin. Keep your shoulders relaxed. Hold for fifteen seconds on each leg.

Seated back of leg stretch seated.

Standing back of leg stretch.

11. Inner Thigh Stretch (thirty seconds)

Sit up straight on the end of a secured chair (one with no wheels), with your legs straight, your feet flexed, and your thighs apart in a V. (Again, don't do this exercise if you have a pain in your public bone.) Put your fists on the seat of the chair behind you by your butt. Hold your transverse in as you stick your butt out for an easy inner thigh stretch. Do not round your upper back as you come forward to get a stretch. Instead, fold forward at your hips keeping your back flat. Hold the stretch for thirty seconds. Do not hold your breath. Remember to count. This stretch can also be done on the floor.

12. Headlifts (four minutes)

It is difficult to work in a back-lying position because gravity makes it harder to engage the transverse muscle in this position. This is why it's easier to strengthen your transverse muscle whenever you feed the baby in a seated position, where gravity is your friend. You should be doing at least 500 transverse exercises per day before you start these headlifts.

Start with a belly breath so that your muscles are out (at the first floor) when you begin the exercise, and in (going from the fifth to the sixth floor) on the work of lifting your head. As I've said before, when you lift your head so that your shoulders come off the floor, it is impossible to hold in your transverse. And as I've said a million times, if you can't hold in your transverse, you shouldn't be doing it! So instead of making the exercise harder by lifting your head higher, you can make it harder by bringing your heels further away from your buttocks. The further away your heels are from your butt, the higher the small of your back comes off the floor. The higher your back comes off the floor, the harder it is to use your abdominals to put it on the floor during the

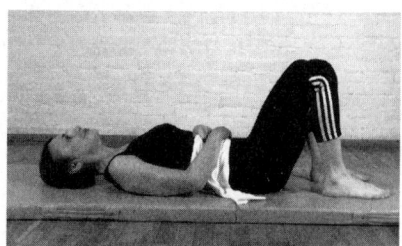

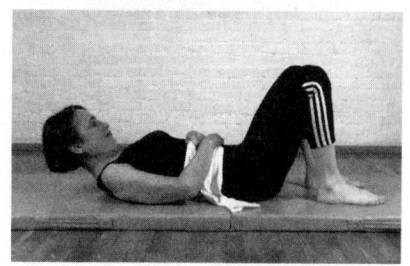

exercise. Remember that promise you made to me at the beginning of the book? So make sure only your head comes off the floor. No shoulders!

Do not jut your chin out when lifting your head. Press the back of your neck to the floor. When you jut you cannot hold your transverse in. Lift your head by nodding "yes." Remember, this is not a crunch or sit-up, this is a headlift! Put your splint around your abdominal separation to hold the two halves of the abdominal muscles together. (If you have a separation at the top, splint at the top under the ribs; if it's in the middle, splint in the middle; and so on.) If you have a diastasis in all three places, do one set in each position, starting with where it is the worst (usually in the middle, at the bellybutton or right above it).

Lying on your back, put the splint under you. Take your left hand and grab the splint on the right side, pulling it toward the middle. Do the same with the other hand on the other side, ending with both hands together resting on your bellybutton or just above it. Relax your arms on the floor.

With knees bent and feet close to your buttocks do these four steps:

a. Expand your belly to the first floor with a belly breath and then bring your transverse to the fifth floor. As it moves back toward your spine, imagine your ribs coming together. Do not use your pelvis while bringing your transverse toward your spine.

b. Hold your transverse at the fifth floor as you imagine your bellybutton zipping up under your ribs. This puts the small of your back on the floor.

c. Think of pulling your ribs together as you pull the splint toward the middle of your body. Continue to hold the splint after you pull it together.

d. Press the back of your neck on the floor, contract your transverse muscle from the fifth to sixth floor as you lift your head, bringing your chin to your chest. Count out loud while doing two sets of 20 repetitions. Hold your transverse at the fifth floor as you put your head back down on the floor.

Keep your eyes closed while doing this exercise so you can concentrate on your transverse muscle. If you don't consciously think about it, you are probably not working it! I like to imagine a wave of light flowing up my back from my bellybutton to my head when going from the fifth to the sixth floor. Imagine this wave of light lifting your head.

It takes about one minute to do 10 headlifts. Remember, you can make this exercise harder by moving your heels away from your buttocks.

13. Abdominal Leg Slides (one minute)

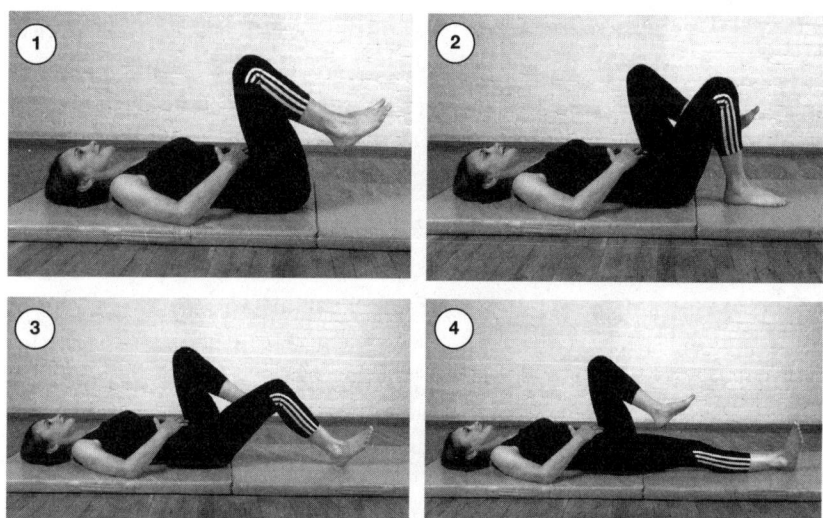

Get into a back-lying position (see my earlier instructions for doing this correctly on page 22). Never roll on your back until your head is touching the ground. Hold your transverse at the fifth floor as you bring both bent knees up in the air. Place one hand on your belly to make sure you are holding your transverse in and the other at your waist by the small of your back, with the palm facing up, to make sure your lower back is on the floor. This is to make sure that your transverse is in and the small of your back is not lifted. Now bring your transverse to the fifth floor and hold it there as you slowly put just one foot on the floor. Then, slowly slide your heel down the floor until your leg is straight. Continue to hold your transverse at the fifth floor while you slowly slide this leg back up toward your buttocks and then lift it back up in the air to the starting position. Now do the same thing with the other leg.

This is harder than it looks. Do this alternating leg slide 15 times. If this is too easy for you, progress to lifting the sliding leg an inch off the floor as you are straightening it and then bring it back up to the starting position. **Note:** If you can't hold your transverse in at the fifth floor while doing this, or if the small of your back is arching up, it's too advanced for you, so please don't do it!

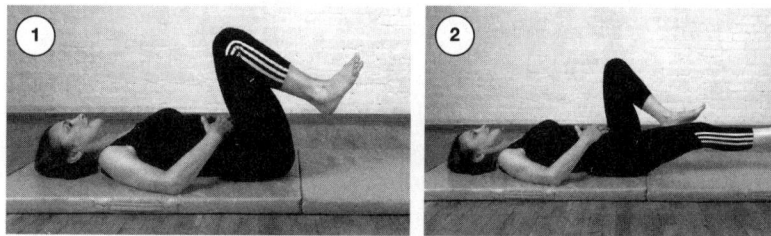

Advanced abdominal leg slides.

14. Obliques (one minute)

Lie on your side with your arm under your head and your feet flexed. You are lined up correctly if you can see your toes. Bring your transverse to the fifth floor and hold it there as you lift your waist up so there is a space between your waist and the floor. Keep your waist lifted in the air and count out loud as you do 10 contractions from the fifth to the sixth floor. Hold your transverse at the fifth floor as you put your waist back on the floor.

Next, bend your knees. Your bottom arm should be resting under your head and your top arm should be bent, with your hand touching your ear. Bring your transverse to the fifth floor. Imagine zipping your bellybutton up under your ribs (as you did with the headlifts). Bring your transverse to the sixth floor as you slowly move your elbow toward your waist. Count out loud while doing 10 repetitions. Your transverse stays at the fifth floor as you slowly bring your head back to the starting position.

Make sure your head faces forward as you lift toward your waist. Do not turn your head toward your waist, as this crossover movement will increase the size of your diastasis. Now sit up correctly and do 10 repetitions of both these exercises on your other side.

15. Seated Military Press (one minute)

Sit on a resistance band on the floor or in a chair. Hold the ends of your band in your hands (the more band you hold in your fists, the harder the exercise). Start with your elbows down by your sides, wrists flat, shoulders lined up with your hips. Take a belly breath and expand your belly to the first floor. Then bring your transverse in to the fifth floor, which is your starting position. Now contract to the sixth floor as you straighten your arms directly up toward the ceiling. Do not bring your hands together. Count out loud as you do two sets of 12 repetitions. Keep your transverse at the fifth floor as you bring your arms back down to the starting position. Think of your abdominals doing the work of lifting your arms. It makes it much easier to work the abs and arms at the same time!

Straighten your arms without locking your elbows, using slow, controlled movements. Do not arch your back.

Note: If you have shoulder problems, lifting your arms overhead with either a resistance band or weights is not a good idea.

Starter's tips: The number of repetitions is not as important as the quality of each movement. If you feel pain, stop and rest before trying to resume the exercise. If the muscle you're contracting feels tired, stop the repetitions even if you have not performed the designated number. If this becomes too easy, make the band shorter or use a resistance band with a stronger resistance.

16. Rowing (one minute)

Sit on the floor with your resistance band under your feet, taking the ends in your hands, with your fingernails in the band and your palms facing each other. Your shoulders should be lined up with your elbows and hips, and your knees should be bent. Hold your transverse at the fifth floor and then move out to the sixth floor as you bring your elbows back. Count out loud as you do two sets of 12 repetitions. Stay at the fifth floor as you bring your arms back to the starting position. Your elbows should not go forward of your shoulders, as that rounds the shoulders. Again, do this using slow, controlled movements.

Starter's tip: With this exercise, digging your fingernails into the band helps to keep your wrists straight. Don't use your wrists to pull the band. The whole forearm moves as one unit. This exercise can also be done while sitting in a chair.

17. Biceps
(one minute)

Hold your resistance band the same way you held it for the rowing exercise, with your palms facing each other. Your shoulders should be lined up with your elbows and your elbows should be glued to your sides during the whole exercise. Bring your transverse to the fifth floor and hold it there. Now go to the sixth floor as you bring both your forearms toward your shoulders and count out loud. Stay at the fifth floor as you slowly bring your arms back to the starting position. Do two sets of 12 repetitions. To make the exercise harder, shorten the band by putting more of it in your hands. This exercise can also be done seated on the floor or in a chair.

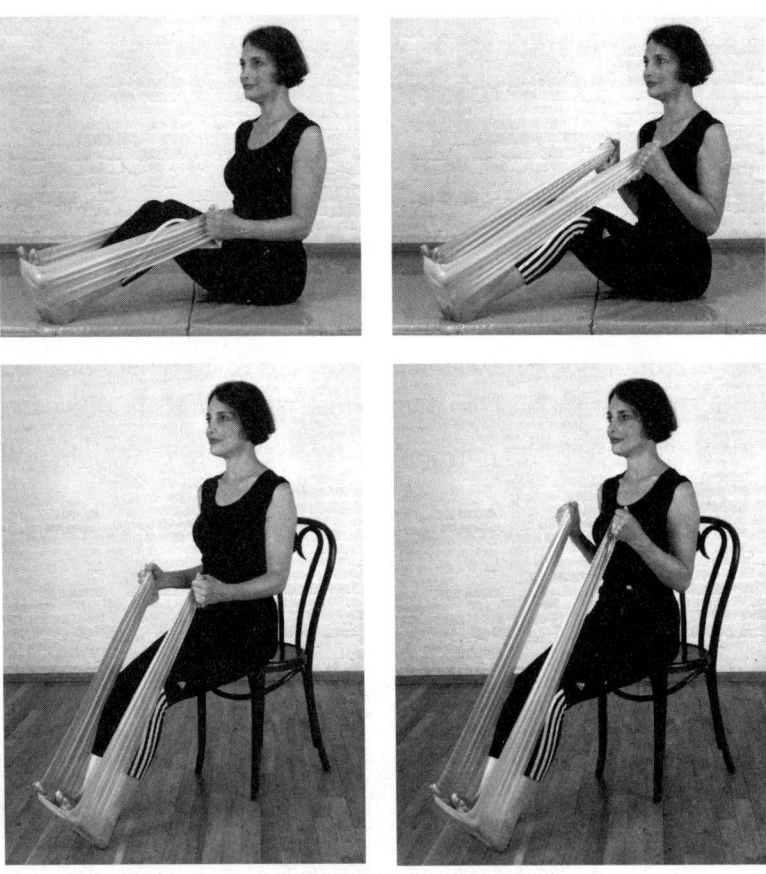

18. Triceps
(one minute)

Sit on a very stable chair (or one that is secured to an immovable object), holding on to either side of the seat. Put your feet far enough in front of you so that your knees are lined up with your ankles. Now hold your transverse in at the fifth floor as you lift your butt up off the seat and in front of the chair. Continue to hold at the

Note: *The chair in the photos is not a secure chair. Make sure you use a secure chair.*

fifth floor as you bring your buttocks down a little below your seat. This is the starting position. Now go from the fifth to the sixth floor, counting as you straighten your arms and bring your buttocks back up to seat level. Make sure your back is touching the front of the chair at all times. Do not arch your back or lock your elbows as you are doing this. Do two sets of 12 repetitions.

19. Chest Press (one minute)

Put your resistance band on your back and under your armpits, holding the ends of the band in your fists with your arms in an L-position. Take a belly breath and bring your transverse to the fifth floor. It stays at the fifth floor for the whole exercise. Slowly

straighten your arms out in front of you without locking your elbows, as if you are punching someone with both fists. Remember to keep your chest wide, shoulders down, relaxed wrists flat, and back straight. Do two sets of 12. Do not bring the arms together on the forward movement, as this

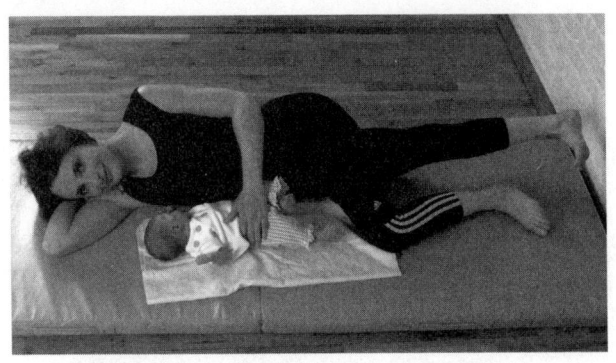

You can feed your baby while doing side lying leg exercises.

rounds the shoulders. Remember, the shorter the band, the more resistance and the harder the exercise.

The next five exercises are done in a side-lying position on the floor. When doing exercises in a side-lying position, it is extremely important that your back stay still. Only your leg or hip should move. Moving your back while doing these exercises not only prevents you from strengthening the correct muscles, it also puts too much strain on your lower back. A good way to tell if you are moving your lower back is to put a small, light, square pillow (approximately 16" x 16") behind your back. The pillow will fall over if you are moving your back.

After you get the hang of these side-lying exercises, you can even try feeding your baby while doing them! Tie a resistance band in a lasso-like knot around your ankles. Start with a diameter of about twelve inches. If this is too difficult, untie the band and make it larger. Do exercises 20 to 23, sit up, do exercise 24, and then repeat exercises 20 to 23 on your other side.

20. Outer Thighs (one minute, thirty seconds on each side)

Tie your resistance band in a knot with a diameter of about twelve inches. Place it around your ankles. Make it bigger it you find it too difficult doing the exercises at this diameter. Using a mat or towel on the floor, lie down on your side with both your knees bent. Place your lower foot against the wall to secure the resistance band. This is very important. You can prop your head up with a pillow if it's more comfortable. Make sure your pelvis is lined up with your hips and you're not leaning back. Keep your transverse at the fifth floor as you lift your top leg straight up until you feel the resistance in the band and the muscle working in the outer thigh.

Keep your foot flexed and your knee facing forward. Hold your leg in this position as you do 10 contractions from the fifth to the sixth floor. Holding the transverse at the fifth floor, touch one knee to the other and then raise your leg back up, continuing to hold your transverse at the fifth floor. Do not let your hip fall backwards on the upward movement. Remember, your back should not move. Do 5 of these. Don't forget to count out loud to ensure you are breathing. End this exercise by holding the transverse in at the fifth floor as you slowly rest the top knee on the bottom knee. Then bring the top knee in front of you so it rests on the floor. Keep your hand on your belly so you know that you are working your abs correctly.

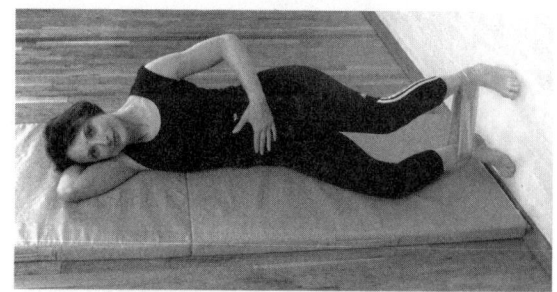

Outer leg stretch: Start by holding your leg in the air.

21. Hamstrings (one minute, thirty seconds on each side)

Keeping the resistance band around your ankles, and the bottom foot on the wall to secure the band, place a pillow between your knees. Hold your transverse in at the fifth floor, and then move it toward your back to the sixth floor as you bring your heel toward your buttocks. Hold it there for a moment and then, keeping the transverse at the fifth floor, slowly bring your heel back to the starting position. Count out loud. Keep your hand on your belly so you know that you are working your abs correctly. Do 12 reps. The knee does not move during this exercise. Remember not to move your back when you bring your heel toward your butt.

Touch the bottom knee with your top knee.

Resting position.

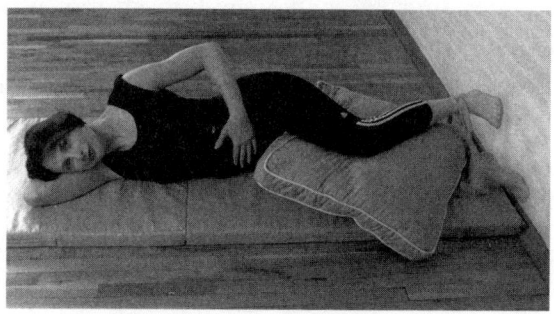

Starting position for hamstring exercise.

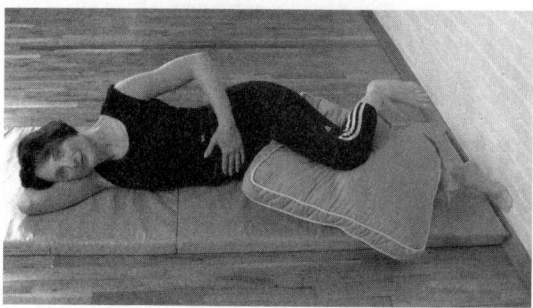

Ending position.

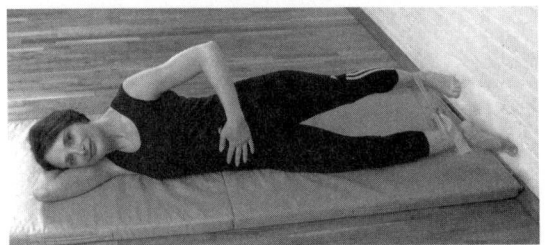

Starting position for buttock exercise.

Ending position.

22. Buttocks (one minute, thirty seconds on each side)

Take the pillow out from between your knees but keep the resistance band around your ankles. Bend your bottom knee. Put just the toes of the foot of bottom leg on the wall. Your top leg should be straight, with a flexed foot, a little behind the bent bottom leg in the starting position. Hold your transverse at the fifth and go to the sixth floor as you move your top leg straight back behind you so you feel it in your butt. This is a very small movement. Hold it there for a moment, then, with your transverse at the fifth floor, slowly bring it back to the starting position. Do not move or arch your back when doing this exercise. Do 12 reps. **Note:** If this exercise is too difficult for you, do it without the resistance band. Keep your hand on your belly so you know you're working your abs correctly.

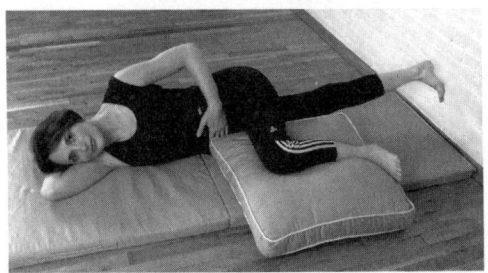

Starting position for inner thigh exercise without resistance band.

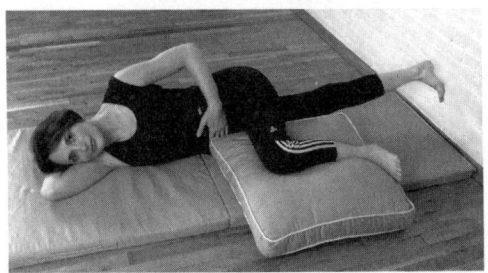

Ending position.

23. Inner Thighs (one minute, thirty seconds on each side)

This exercise is done initially without the resistance band, in the side-lying position on the floor. You can always use the band if you want to make the exercise harder. In this exercise, the bottom foot is not touching the wall. Take the knee of the top leg and place it on the floor in front of you on a pillow. The bottom leg is straight, with the foot flexed. If you cannot see your toes, then move your leg forward. Hold the transverse in at the fifth floor as you lift the bottom leg in the air, with your knee facing forward (not up). Hold it there with your transverse at

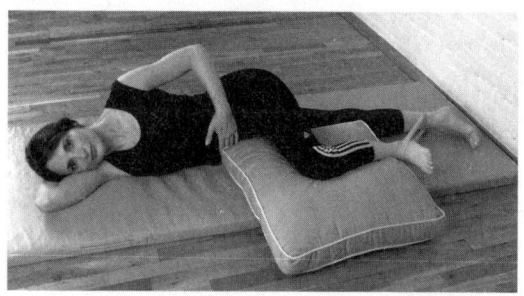

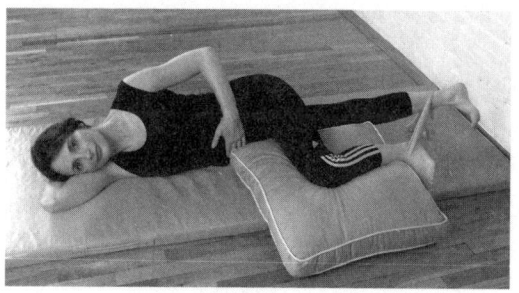

*Starting position for inner thigh exercise
with resistance band.*

Ending position.

the fifth floor as you count out loud to ten. Now contract your abs from the fifth to the sixth floor on the upward movement of lifting your leg. Count out loud as you do 5 of these little lifts. Keeping your transverse in at the fifth floor, slowly put your leg back on the floor. Again, remember not to move your back on the upward movement of your leg. Put your hand on your belly so you know you're working the abs correctly.

24. Quad Strengthening
(one minute, thirty seconds on each side)

Holding your transverse at the fifth floor, bring yourself to a sitting position, and put the band back around your ankles (if you took it off during the last exercise). Place one foot on the band and wrap the other side of the band around your other ankle. Put

*Starting position for quad strengthening
with resistance band.*

Ending position.

both hands behind the knee of the leg you are working and sit up straight. Hold your transverse at the fifth floor. Now go to the sixth floor as you slowly straighten your leg. Hold the leg there for a moment. Then, keeping the transverse at the fifth floor, slowly bring it back to the starting position. Change legs. Do 12 reps on each side.

Get back into a side-lying position on the other side so you can do the outer thigh, hamstrings, buttocks, and inner thigh exercises on that side.

25. Lower Back Stretch with Breathing and Relaxation (one-and-a-half minutes)

From a side-lying position without lifting your head, keep your transverse at the fifth floor while you roll onto your back. Put your arms on the floor by your sides and bend your knees, bringing your heels close to your buttocks. Holding the transverse at the fifth floor, keep your feet on the floor and roll your knees to one side. Then look over the opposite shoulder. Close your eyes and breathe through this stretch. Expand your belly and exhale as you visualize the release of the muscles in your neck, shoulders, and back. Relax and let all your muscles go soft as Jell-O. Take forty-five breaths. Now hold your transverse at the fifth floor, keeping your feet on the floor, and roll your knees to the other side. Look over your shoulder in the opposite direction. Breathe through the stretch another forty-five times. If you bring your heels away from your buttocks while you are doing this stretch, you will feel it more in your upper back.

Post(partum) Script

AS IMPORTANT AS IT IS to get back into shape and to get at least some of your old life back, I want you to literally give yourself a break from time to time. If labor is like a marathon, parenthood is a perpetual race. So I am encouraging you to baby yourself, especially during the first year after childbirth. To that end, I offer you the following suggestions that have worked for other moms:

Get a babysitter. New moms can be crazed about leaving freshly popped infants in the hands of anyone but themselves ("No one knows better than me how to care for my child," the credo goes). For heaven's sake, let that newborn go. Hand the baby off to your partner, mother, mother-in-law, or any other trustworthy friend or family member who volunteers, or get a babysitter so you can do something or absolutely nothing! Even an hour respite can be an hour of pure bliss.

Get a pedicure. Speaking of bliss, my co-author, Jodie, treated herself to a monthly pedicure after her baby was born. This treatment includes a hot foot soak, a leg massage, and polished toes. You can even catch some Zs while you're waiting for your nails to dry. If you feel the need for some handholding, get a manicure, too.

Sleep whenever you can. In this case, don't do what my co-author Jodie did, which was clean the house and write e-mails while her baby napped. Let the chores go begging, enlist some help with the domestic drudgery, and sleeeeep.

Exercise your brain. One of the biggest complaints voiced by new moms is that their baby-centric life is filled with nothing but poop, pumping, binkys (where's the binky?!), and naps. Although you probably won't have the time or energy to read a book cover to cover, or even a newspaper for that matter, make sure you do something to stimulate your brain. You can start a book-on-tape club with other mothers, take your sleeping baby on a stroll through your local museum, or, if your town has one, go to a matinee at a movie theatre that caters to moms and their infants. Loews Theatres has a program called Reel Moms, and it's a blast.

Get a mommy sponsor. Hello, my name is fill-in-the-blank, and I'm a new mother. Borrowing from the 12-step paradigm, have a list of three people you can call when you're feeling as though having a baby was the dumbest decision you ever made in your life. We all go through it (though not all of us are honest enough to admit it), and we all need some emotional support when colic raises its ugly head or postpartum blues get us by the throat. Don't be ashamed, call someone to complain. If you're really spinning out of control, call a professional therapist or psychiatrist. There are medications you can take even while breast-feeding.

Don't neglect your partner. If you are a single mom, you are free to devote all your attention to the baby. If you're not, be careful not to ignore the one who helped make that baby in the first place. New moms often put baby blinders on as a result of feeling overwhelmed by the magnitude of being caretaker and nurturer. You need to come up for air sometime, and when you do, don't forget to throw a little love in your partner's direction.

I'd love to hear from all you moms out there, so please feel free to write me via the Maternal Fitness Web site (www.maternalfitness.com) if you have any questions, to order a video or DVD, or to sign up for one of my "Lose Your Mummy Tummy" seminars. Let me know how you are progressing. If you want to send me a "before" and "after" picture of your tummy, I'll put it in my scrapbook! You can also write to me at:

Maternal Fitness
108 E. 16th Street (4th floor)
New York, NY 10003

Acknowledgments

THIS BOOK IS THE RESULT of a collaboration between many people and could not have been accomplished without their support, guidance, encouragement, and inspiration.

I am indebted to the many pregnant women and new moms with whom I've had the honor to work over the past fourteen years. They allowed me to practice, develop, and hone my craft; have been gracious enough to let me stick my fingers in their bellybuttons; and have taught me so much about diastasis and life after birth! I would especially like to thank Maternal Fitness graduate Wendy Friedmann and her beautiful blue-eyed daughter Melanie, who was one of our models.

I am also indebted to:

my co-writer, Jodie Gould, a talented writer with a great sense of humor who magically took my words and ideas and created this wonderful book. She made the experience of writing a book fun!

my hard-working literary agent, Linda Konner, who just happens to be a wonderful matchmaker, as evidenced by her pairing me with my co-writer, Jodie Gould, and my publisher, Da Capo!

my editor, Marnie Cochran, who was always available, knowledgeable, and enthusiastic about my book. Her clarity and insights have made publishing a book a true pleasure.

I owe a great deal to my dear friend Annie Watt for all her help, interest, and encouragement along the way.

Also, MG Vander Elst for her beautiful photographs.

Kevin Pyle for his wonderful illustrations.

Holly Herman for writing one of my favorite books, *How to Raise Children without Breaking Your Back,* and for letting me use some of her exercises in my book!

My two sisters, Susan and Sharon, for their love and support, and my daughter, Flo, for posing in many photos and for sleeping through the night so I could work on this book!

–Julie Tupler

Thanks to my co-author, Julie Tupler, for her vision, energy, and good humor and for helping me get rid of my mummy tummy! To my dear friend and agent, Linda Konner, for always finding a winning project and for always having my best interests in mind. To Marnie Cochran, who is both a talented editor and a delight to work with. And to the Da Capo art, sales, and marketing folks for their creativity and support.

–Jodie Gould

Index

Abdominal exercises. *See also* Cross over situps; Crunches; Tupler Technique
    contractions, 18–19
    crossover, 97
    elevators, 18
    fetus and, xv
    timeline of, 16–17
    transverse muscles as missing link in, 3

Abdominal muscles. *See also* Obliques; Rectus abdominis; Transverse muscles
    back support from strengthening, xi
    decreased separation caused by growing uterus, xv
    three sets of, 2
    Tupler Technique exercises using transverse, xiii
    after uterus reduces, 1

Adhesions
    from episiotomy, 51–52
    preventing/treating, 51–52
    scar massage for, 52
    symptoms of, 51

Aerobics
    resuming, 96–97
    shoes for, 97

Anatomy
    as destiny, 2–4

Anesthesia
    for tummy tucks, 57, 59

Ankles
    circling for, 75
    exercises for, 75–76
    shoes supporting, 97
    swollen, 75
    toe lifting for, 76

Baby Bjorn, 12

Baby carriers
    backpack, 88–89
    exercise for, 89
    front loading, 88
    slings as, 89
    splint use with, 88

ball rolling for, 74
exercises for, 73–75
flat, 70
heel lifting for, 75
insoles/arch supports for pain in, 73
size increase from pregnancy of, 72
toe curl for, 73
toe grabbing exercise for, 75
towel grabbing for, 74
Femina cones, 56
Fissures
  from breast-feeding, 53
Floor abdominizers, 8

Goodman, Debra, 57
Gravity
  on crunches, 7
Groceries
  lifting, 93
  technique for, 93

Headlifts
  in fifteen-minute Tupler workout,
    37–38
  instruction for, 20–21, *21, * 37
Hemorrhoids
  after labor, 50
Herman, Hollis, 63
High chairs
  putting children in, 90
Hormones. *See also* Relaxin hormone
  bones and, 81
  in initial stage after delivery, 12
*How to Raise Children without Breaking Your
  Back* (Herman), 63
Huffing, 47

Ice packs
  for episiotomy recovery, 51

ICEA. *See* International Childbirth
    Education Association
Incontinence
  Kegels help with, 25, 54
  pelvic floor muscles' restoration helping
    with risk of, xi
  types of, 54
Injury
  preventing, xi
Intercourse
  baby's napping and, 96
  painful, 95
  six week wait before, 95
International Childbirth Education
    Association (ICEA), xiv

Joints. *See also* Wrists
  exercises for, 64–76
  laxity from relaxin hormone, 32
  strengthening/protecting, 63
  as vulnerable, 63

Kegel, Arnold, 25
Kegels
  elevators, 26
  after episiotomy, 51
  in fifteen-minute Tupler workout, 33
  incontinence helped by, 25, 54
  during nursing, 18
  sexual pleasure enhanced by, 25
  ten-second hold, 26
  urinating and, 25
Kinesiotape, 49
Knees
  exercises for, 70–72
  as hinge, 70
  leg kick exercise for, 70–71
  in pregnancy, 69

conditions, 54, 65

episiotomy recovery caused pain reduced by engaging, 51

function of, 3–4

identifying, 25

incontinence helped with restoration of, xi

pregnancy as weakening, 25

relaxing, x

restoring tone of, xi

squatting as stretching for, 27

Pelvic tilt

instruction for, 19–20

Perineum. *See also* Episiotomies

tearing of, 50

Pessaries, 56

Physical activity

of postpartum women, 11

Pilates

core abdominal muscles worked by, 98

exercises to avoid in, 98

machines, 98

Pinched nerve. *See* Thoracic outlet syndrome

Pirie, Alex, 63

Play yards

lifting baby out of, 90

Postpartum recovery

physical activity during, 11

Tupler Technique as helping with, xv

Posture, 63–64

Pregnancy

feet size as increased after, 72

knees during, 69

muscle imbalances after, 98

preparing for future, xiv

thoracic outlet syndrome caused by, 64

Tupler Technique for healthier, xi

Pubic bone separation

belly breaths for, 58

indicators of, 56

pelvis binding with, 58

treatment of, 56

Pubococcygeus (PC)

identifying, 25

as pelvic floor's main muscle, 4, *4*

Purses, 92

Pushing

Tupler Technique abdominal exercises for, ix, xiii

Recovery. *See also* Postpartum recovery

from cesarean, 46–49

as easier with Tupler Technique, xi

from episiotomies, 50–52

from tearing, 51–52

from tummy tuck, 59, 61

Rectus abdominis

anatomy of, 2, *2*

Reel Moms, 120

Relaxin hormone

in body for six months after birth, 63

joint laxity from, 32

linea alba as affected by, 2

Resistance bands

cleaning, 13–14

lifting overhead of, 111

outer thigh exercise with, 43

tips for, 13

toe lifting with, 76

Rowing

instruction for, 40, *40*

Sacroiliac pain

exercises for, 58, 60–62

leg pulls for, 61

inner thighs, *30,* 30–31, 36

lower back, 44

muscles lengthened through,
    28–29, 99

neck, 33

open leg, 99

relaxing body through, 28

standing hip flexor, 36

static, 29

strengthening and, 32

wrists, 69

Stroller Size, 96

Stroller Strides, 96

Strollers

height of, 91

lifting baby out of, 91

putting child in, 91

steps and, 92

types of, 91–92

Swelling

in wrists, 66–67

Swimming

avoid frog kick when, 97

Swings

lifting baby out of, 90–91

as mothers helper, 90

Tantrums

carrying during, 87

Tearing

of perineum, 50

recovery from, 51–52

Teeth

brushing, 80

Telephones

hands-free, 92

TENS. *See* Transcutaneous Electrical
    Nerve Stimulations

Thighs

exercise for outer, 43

press, 43

stretching inner, *30,* 30–31,
    36

Thoracic outlet syndrome

pregnancy caused, 64

Toys

picking up, 88

Transcutaneous Electrical Nerve
    Stimulations (TENS)

for cesarean recovery, 47

Transverse muscles

anatomy of, 2

bowel movement use of, 8

in crunches, 7

exercising for muscles by working, 3

head lifted high during, 7–8

holding in, 78

locating, 16

as missing link in abdominal
    exercises, 3

mummy tummy rid by working,
    3

protracted position of, 8

pushing with, ix

Trapezius muscle

tension in, 64

Tummy tuck

anesthesia used for, 57, 59

candidates for, 55

diastasis surgery v., 5–6

after getting, 59

look after, 61

planning for, 57

procedure for, 55, 59

recovery from, 59, 61

risks of, 55, 57

Waistline
  smaller, xiv
Walking, 96
Welles Step, 27
Wrists. *See also* Carpal tunnel syndrome
  bag lift for, 68
  biking and, 99
  carrying as hard on, 85
  in cradling gesture, 67
  exercises for, 68–69

finger lifts for, 68
learning stretch for, 69
squeeze for, 69
swelling in, 66–67
Yoga and, 97–98

Yoga, 96. *See also* Pilates
  avoid positions in, 97–98
  stress release through, 98
  wrists in, 98

Notes

*Please use these "notes" pages to record your
thoughts, observations, and progress while using the
Tupler Technique to lose your mummy tummy.*